"Frank Pisch keeps his promise to tell stories from his forty-year career as a fundraising consultant to nonprofit leaders. His stories are highly informative and inspiring. They engage us in the importance of building relationships and ask critical questions that must be answered before and during a campaign. Frank adds a model of blending science and art that leads to success. Other sections of *The Spirit of Philanthropy*, such as 'Building a Team' and 'The Perfect Ask,' add to our learning in fascinating ways. We gain further from Frank's reflections on his leadership of the company he founded nearly thirty years ago. It's easy to grasp why The Compass Group is such a nationally valued consulting firm."

## EDWARD J. TOMEY
*Leadership consultant and coach*

"In *The Spirit of Philanthropy*, a highly engaging narrative, Frank Pisch brings into clear focus both the art and science of fundraising. Drawing upon his four decades as a leader in fundraising consulting, Pisch weaves together strategies, anecdotes, wise counsel, and, yes, spirit to offer nonprofit leaders 'bread for the journey' as they position their organizations for robust financial health."

## JIM LEONARD
*Head of school, Santa Fe Preparatory School, 1999–2020*

"For nonprofit leaders, this book will become *the* outstanding and trusted reference for fundraising as you navigate the ever-changing world of philanthropy. Frank Pisch brings the *values of this business* to life in a realistic and simplified way that speaks from the heart even as he provides the technical information to help us all succeed in fundraising for our organizations. It's all here: the why and the how."

LISA DARLING
*Head of school, The Awty International School*


"*The Spirit of Philanthropy*, which is infused with Frank's warm-hearted and intelligent approach to fundraising, provides great insight into how to form relationships with donors and what it takes for donors to make a meaningful difference. In an increasingly competitive and complex philanthropic world, Frank provides the guiding light."

GREG AVIS
*Managing partner, Bangtail Partners; philanthropist and impact investor*

# THE SPIRIT

## OF

# PHILANTHROPY

*Fundraising for a Better World*

# THE SPIRIT

## —— OF ——

# PHILANTHROPY

*Fundraising for a Better World*

# FRANK PISCH

*Advantage* | Books

Published by Advantage, Charleston, South Carolina.
Member of Advantage Media.

ADVANTAGE is a registered trademark, and the Advantage colophon is a trademark of Advantage Media Group, Inc.

Printed in the United States of America.

10  9  8  7  6  5  4  3  2  1

ISBN: 978-1-64225-548-5 (Paperback)
ISBN: 978-1-64225-793-9 (Hardcover)
ISBN: 978-1-64225-547-8 (eBook)

LCCN: 2022914073

Cover design by Hampton Lamoreux.
Layout design by Amanda Haskin.

This publication is designed to provide accurate and authoritative information in regard to the subject matter covered. It is sold with the understanding that the publisher is not engaged in rendering legal, accounting, or other professional services. If legal advice or other expert assistance is required, the services of a competent professional person should be sought.

Advantage Media helps busy entrepreneurs, CEOs, and leaders write and publish a book to grow their business and become the authority in their field. Advantage authors comprise an exclusive community of industry professionals, idea-makers, and thought leaders. Do you have a book idea or manuscript for consideration? We would love to hear from you at **AdvantageMedia.com**.

## THIS BOOK IS DEDICATED TO:

*My children, Mark, Sallie, and Annie Rose, who*
*were always enamored by the work I do.*

*Kathleen, my North Star and my rock, for always believing in me.*

*Rob, Beth, the Compass team, and our clients, all of whom are doing*
*their best work every day to help make the world a better place.*

# CONTENTS

"The two most important times in your life are the day you are born and the day you discover why."

—MARK TWAIN

# INTRODUCTION

Over the years, I've told many people, "I have the greatest job in the world, because I get up every day and go to work with people who are trying to make this world a better place."

This is a book of thoughts on how I view the profession of fundraising consulting, the philosophy that I think is important, and the values that are imbued in the work of my company, The Compass Group.

I'm not a fundraiser; I'm an experiential educator. I don't fundraise for clients of The Compass Group; I teach them how to do it well so they can do it on their own. As a matter of fact, my first job was as a teacher.

## Powerful Inspiration

In the early 1970s, I graduated with a BA degree from the School of Education at the University of Connecticut and got a job teaching Biology and English at South Catholic High School in Hartford, Connecticut. While in that job, I was inspired by an article called

"Walkabout" by Maurice Gibbons for *Phi Delta Kappan* magazine in 1974.[1]

This award-winning article would serve as a guidepost for my professional life.

It was the story of Aborigines in Australia and how they determined whether a young person in their tribe was ready to be considered an adult—a contributing member of their society.

As the story goes, the elders of the tribe would send a teenager out on a forty-day walkabout into the forbidding Australian outback. If that young person survived and returned safe and sound, he or she had proven they had what it takes to be a contributing member of the tribe. This story emphasized the vital importance of determination and self-reliance in Aboriginal culture.

The article brought several questions to my mind: What factors would determine if an individual was a contributing member of society in our culture? What skill sets are needed to achieve that status? How do we acquire those skill sets?

# Adventure Challenge

I set out to find some answers. I became involved in discussions with a number of experiential educators: Dave Mellen, creator of Experience It; Sister Maryann Hedaa, an experiential educator who developed a program at St. Mary's Academy called Adventure Challenge; Keith King, who operated LIVE (Learning in Vigorous Environments) at Keene State College; Josh Minor, Joe Nold, Peter Willauer, and John Huey with Outward Bound; Paul Petzoldt, founder of the National Outdoor Leadership School; and a variety of professionals with the Association for Experiential Education.

---

1    Maurice Gibbons, "Walkabout," *Phi Delta Kappan* (May 1974).

With the help of those experts, I identified three essential skills for becoming a contributing member of our society: the ability to learn, the ability to relate to others, and the ability to make responsible decisions. This led to the founding, incorporation, and funding of the Adventure Challenge School in Manchester, Connecticut.

Adventure Challenge was based on three principles:

» Students would get a hands-on approach to the subjects they learned in class so they could make the connection between academics and experience—the beginning of a real education.

» Students would participate in an adventure experience—backpacking, camping, rock climbing, caving, sailing, or an urban immersion—to challenge themselves, build self-confidence, and learn to work as a team.

» Students, as a group, would participate in a service project in their hometown to give back to their community.

The Adventure Challenge School was a very popular and successful program back in the '70s. It was featured in local newspapers and on local and national television. In spite of this success, the board of Adventure Challenge closed its doors in the early '80s because the school ran out of money.

## A Commitment to Fundraising

I was stunned and disappointed by the closing of Adventure Challenge, and I decided that no nonprofit worth its salt should close because of a lack of funding. It was clear that fundraising was a skill I needed to acquire.

While running Adventure Challenge, I was awarded a fellowship to Antioch New England Graduate School, and I obtained a master's degree in organization and management, specializing in nonprofit institutions. This gave me the opportunity to do pro bono work for the International Center for Endangered Species in Newport, Rhode Island, where I ran into a man named Ralph Peterson of Ketchum Inc. Headquartered in Pittsburgh, Ketchum was the largest fundraising consulting firm in the world.

Ralph introduced me to fundraising consulting "Ketchum-style." The company focused on helping nonprofits obtain the resources they needed to fulfill their missions and ensure their sustainability—exactly the skills I was looking for. When I accepted an offer to join the firm in 1984, my entire career path changed.

> No nonprofit worth its salt should close because of a lack of funding.

Working at Ketchum was a revelation. I spent my days with the team who founded the profession of fundraising consulting, and they taught me how it was done. It wasn't easy. Ketchum put me through an intense training program of classroom learning, then sent me out into the field with a veteran consultant.

## On-the-Job Training

The classroom learning was important, but at Ketchum, you learned mostly by doing, working on-site at a client's location day after day, and gradually being given more responsibility.

One of the first clients I worked with was a YMCA in Framingham, Massachusetts, under the tutelage of Jeffrey Wolfman. I went on to consult at Wilson College, a small, private women's college, then to large public universities such as the University of Minnesota, where I was part of the largest fundraising campaign any public university in America had undertaken.

My experience at Ketchum gave me direct exposure to the business of fundraising and the skills and confidence to be a hands-on fundraiser for several nonprofits: Berry College in Rome, Georgia; the Association of Governing Boards of Universities and Colleges in Washington, DC; and the Baltimore Symphony Orchestra.

Although the time I spent as a fundraiser deepened my understanding of philanthropy, consulting was often in my thoughts. I craved the opportunity to combine what I was learning every day with who I was as an educator to help nonprofits across the country.

With this in mind, in 1997 I returned to consulting and rejoined Ketchum, which was under new ownership and headquartered in Dallas. I believed I could be part of taking the company to a whole new level, and I was excited to work again with the professionals who stayed with Ketchum through the transition.

## A Better Way

During my second stint with Ketchum, I thought there had to be a better way to advise nonprofits on fundraising. I envisioned a model that put consultants and clients side by side, working in partnership to customize fundraising programs and craft strategies to meet the specific needs of nonprofits.

For me, the priority was teaching clients how to fundraise on their own. As we strengthened their ability to accomplish the day-to-day tasks of fundraising—and boosted their confidence—we would build their capacity as fundraisers.

Ideally, when our time with an organization ended, they wouldn't need us anymore—our goal would be to educate them to the point where we put ourselves out of a job.

This philosophy inspired the founding of my own company, The Compass Group Inc. As Compass grew, I envisioned a series of "walkabout goals" for our clients:

» They create aspirational visions for their organizations.

» They build the capacity to be sustainable over time.

» They build teams that are invested and engaged in fundraising.

» They create lifelong relationships with their donors.

» They make a difference in the world.

I continue to be committed to teaching, mentoring, and coaching nonprofits as they work to achieve these goals.

# The Power of Storytelling

As an educator, I've often explored ways in which different lessons can be taught and learned. I've discovered storytelling can be effective, interesting, and fun if the student is willing and engaged. I assume if you're reading this book, you're willing and engaged, so I'm going to rely on storytelling to share my perspective.

But please keep in mind the stories in this book are mine. They're my personal recollections of people I knew and situations I was involved in during my career. I've tried to be as accurate as possible in relating these stories, but in the end, they are my recollections.

"Philanthropy, charity, giving voluntarily and freely ... call it what you like, but it is truly a jewel of an American tradition."

—JOHN F. KENNEDY

# CHAPTER 1

# THE SPIRIT OF PHILANTHROPY

Philanthropy isn't about money.

You might be surprised to hear me say that. After all, I've been either a fundraising consultant or fundraiser for more than forty years, and I've secured more than $4 billion in philanthropic support for nonprofit organizations. Throughout my career, however, it has become clear: *philanthropy is about inspiration and impact.*

## Inspiration and Impact

*"Giving is not about making a gift, it's about making a difference."*

—Kathy Calvin, CEO,
United Nations Foundation

Philanthropy is often inspired by visionary leaders. Here's a story that will show you what I mean. The Boys Industrial School in Mount Berry, Georgia, was founded in 1902 by Martha Berry, whose vision was to provide education for poor boys in Northwest Georgia. When Martha visited the home of inventor Thomas Edison and his wife Mina, the course of the school changed forever.

Edison introduced Berry to entrepreneur Henry Ford. At that time, Ford was the richest man in America and the richest industrialist in the world. As Berry described her vision for Berry College, Ford became intrigued by the fact that students at the school not only received an education but gained practical, hands-on life experience: they built their own dorms and classroom buildings, plowed the fields, grew their own food, and held jobs to work their way through college.

Ford envisioned the underprivileged students getting a great education, landing good jobs after graduation, and improving not only their own quality of life but also their struggling families' as well. The first gifts he made to the school were tractors and a truck.

Ford wanted to help Berry pursue her mission to give students better lives, and he had the financial means to do so. Inspired by her vision and dedication, he donated $6 million to the school in the early 1920s. A staggering sum in those days, it allowed Berry

> Rumor has it that Martha Berry was quite creative in her efforts to engage and cultivate the Fords. Local residents tell tales of fresh-baked apple pies delivered hot from Berry College to the Fords' train every time it stopped in Rome, Georgia, for fuel and water, en route between Michigan and Florida.

to buy twenty-nine thousand acres of land, making the school the largest college campus in the world.

Ford then brought in Italian masons to build magnificent stone buildings on this land—now known as the Ford Campus—and he was instrumental in the construction of the Water Wheel at the Old Mill. In 1926 the Boys Industrial School became Berry College, where those landmarks still stand today.

Ford was inspired by Martha Berry and her vision. He believed in her and saw a role for himself in making that vision a reality. He was inspired to make a difference that not only transformed the campus and the students but transformed him as well.

---

*"What the Fords gave of themselves was worth more to the schools than what they gave of their means."*

—*Martha Berry*

---

Philanthropy can also be inspired by a visionary donor. Take the story of the Davis United World College (UWC) Scholars Program. Inspired by the United World Colleges movement—which brings students together from all over the world to live and learn during their last two years of high school in one of seventeen locations on five continents—Shelby Davis and Phil Geier created the Scholars Program based on a single idea:

If you could bring thousands of talented students from every corner of the globe to US colleges and universities, you could create international understanding and change the world.

This idea reinforced Davis's personal and professional experiences and inspired a vision for impacting the future. He explained: "When I started my business career, I took my own history lesson from Princeton: I learned how leaders make a difference, in their countries, in their centuries. So I invested in leaders, and that investment helped me to be successful. I'm looking to invest again in leaders of the future."[2]

Today, the Davis UWC Scholars Program partners with nearly a hundred US colleges and universities to provide annual grants that support need-based scholarships for each matriculated UWC graduate for up to four years of undergraduate study. It's currently the largest undergraduate scholarship program in the world. And Shelby Davis invests $40–$50 million per year to advance his vision for world-changing leadership.

## Reasons for Giving

---

*"In the first thirty years of your life, you should learn, the second thirty years you should earn, and the rest of your life you should return."*

*—Shelby Davis*

---

Donors give for a variety of reasons. Some strongly believe that it's simply the right thing to do. Some believe it's their moral obligation

---

2    Shelby Davis, "Why UWC," September 23, 2017, https://www.davisuwcscholars.org/founders/vision/shelby-davis-explains-why-uwc-.

to support organizations that serve humanity or the environment. Some donors, who have benefited from the philanthropy of others, give to "pay it forward." And others give because it's family tradition.

Regardless of their motivation for giving, the one common thread I've found in my interactions with donors is inspiration and impact. Donors want to be inspired to give to nonprofits that have an impact, and, now more than ever, donors want to be engaged in an organization's mission. They want to feel they're an important part of it, and they want to see how their contributions make a difference.

In Martha Berry's vision for Berry College, Henry Ford found values that reflected his own, and by investing in her vision, he fulfilled his desire to perpetuate those values.

Shelby Davis and Phil Geier created their own vision for the UWC Scholars Program that was embraced by their US higher education partners. That inspiration, combined with the financial means to have transformational impact, helped to make education, as Shelby and Phil put it, "a force to unite peoples, nations, and cultures for peace and a sustainable future."[3]

When a donor feels connected to an organization's mission and sees that their support made great things happen, he or she has given what the Ketchum folks used to call "money without regret."

---

3    Ibid.

# The Magic of Hard Work

*"Great things come from hard work and perseverance. No excuses."*

*—Kobe Bryant*

I always keep in mind that fundraising is a service profession.

Fundraising isn't a job, and it isn't a career—it's a lifestyle. It's a life of service, obligation, and stewardship. Fundraisers give themselves over to missions, values, and goals that are bigger than they are. They make the world a better place by providing resources for institutions that educate, heal, inspire, and help people. I'm fascinated by the magic they create every day.

> **Fundraising isn't a job, and it isn't a career—it's a lifestyle.**

There can be magic in fundraising, but it's magic that occurs only through hard work, preparation, and planning. Many people aren't aware of this. A few years ago, after conducting a successful $5 million solicitation, a dean at a major university medical center said to me, "That was easy. What do I need a development office for?"

After I showed him the thirty-six-month cultivation plan that the university had implemented to develop a solid relationship with the donor—a plan that put the donor in a position to say yes when asked—he began to understand the huge amount of hard work that went into his moment of success.

Fundraisers stand at the intersection of inspiration and impact. Through hard work, they provide opportunities for organizations and donors to come together in *the spirit of philanthropy* to make a difference.

As a fundraising consultant, I'm proud to stand shoulder to shoulder with fundraisers as they work to make the world a better place. They spark the spirit of philanthropy, and that spirit is embodied in a well-planned, efficiently executed fundraising campaign that is a seamless blend of art and science.

*"Comparing the capacity of computers to the capacity of the human brain, I've often wondered, where does our success come from? The answer is synthesis, the ability to combine creativity and calculation, art and science, into a whole that is much greater than the sum of its parts."*

—CHESS CHAMPION
GARRY KASPAROV

CHAPTER 2

# THE ART AND SCIENCE OF FUNDRAISING

Throughout my career, I've often heard the phrase "fundraising is an art and a science." That always made a great deal of sense to me.

I see value in explaining the art and science for those seeking to infuse both in the fundraising process. The process is the daily work of fundraisers and a development office. It's a continual process that, when well executed, will have a powerful impact on both the organization and the donor.

## Balanced but Not Equal

The success of any fundraising effort requires a balance of both art and science. That balance, however, is rarely equal. At the most basic level, the balance is usually influenced by one thing: prospect potential.

Direct-response campaigns that seek small contributions from a large number of donors rely heavily on "science." The who, what, when, where, why, and how of those solicitations are calculated based on internal and external data, statistics, and testing. That's not to say that "artistry" isn't critical in presenting a succinct case for support that triggers action from a large number of prospects, but in these types of campaigns, "science" drives the strategy for soliciting prospects.

Campaigns that focus on securing large gifts from a small number of prospects require a greater degree of "art." While the "science" of identifying and qualifying prospects is still critical in these campaigns, the relationship between the prospect and the organization will have a big impact on fundraising success. Developing relationships requires creativity. In these types of campaigns, "art" drives the strategy for soliciting prospects.

## The Fundraising Cycle

*"If you consider the fundraising cycle to be the Science, then the movement of prospects and donors through that cycle is unquestionably the Art."*

—Kathleen Gaines, senior vice president, The Compass Group

The fundraising process can be illustrated as a cycle that donors move through continuously. The balance between the art and science of fundraising shifts during this cycle:

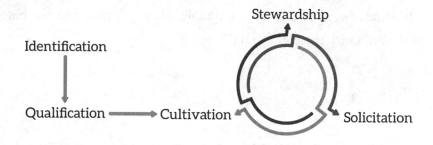

The ultimate goal of the first two steps of this cycle—Identification and Qualification—is to create a pipeline of prospects who can provide donations in support of a nonprofit organization. Potential donors are identified—whether they're individuals, corporations, or foundations—and then qualified to determine the level of gift they can provide if they're properly cultivated, solicited, and stewarded.

Building a pipeline requires a more "scientific" approach that relies on data, research, and other tools and technologies. Implementing these steps can be impersonal, but if they aren't properly executed, fundraising productivity can be undermined.

Executing the cultivation, solicitation, and stewardship phases of the process requires a level of "artistry." This is where it becomes personal, where the quality of the relationship between a donor and an organization will directly influence fundraising.

There's no tried-and-true formula for building these relationships—they'll be as unique as each prospect—but the fundraisers who do it well build a team of internal and external partners; design a strategy to inform and engage prospects over time; regularly adjust to meet the prospect where they are; and make progress in a thoughtful, consistent way.

I've often heard people say the hardest part of fundraising is getting a prospect to become a donor for the first time, but I believe the real work of fundraising is building a relationship that engenders a lifetime of support. Those sustainable relationships reflect the best of the art and science of fundraising.

## The Art

*Art = The expression or application of human creative skill and imagination*

*—Oxford English Dictionary*

We've all been contacted by telephone and/or mail with a request for charitable support. In these instances, fundraising is a basic transaction. This type of approach, no matter how well executed, may get results but leaves many people, even those who donate, feeling empty—like they're just another name on a list. They're left without a deep or lasting connection to the organization, its mission, and its staff, and there's a good chance they won't donate again.

**To be a great artist in this profession, you have to be thoughtful, creative, attentive, empathetic, adaptable, and assertive.**

There's a vastly different way to perform the craft—let's call it the art—of fundraising. In its noblest, most truly philanthropic form, fundraising isn't about money; it's about people and relationships. It's personal.

The highest form of fundraising strives to achieve a vitally important goal, which is to *put the donor first*.

To be a great artist in this profession, you have to be thoughtful, creative, attentive, empathetic, adaptable, and assertive.

Great fundraisers don't focus on numbers; they focus on engaging their donors, involving them in ways that let them know they're making a big difference for an organization—making something wonderful happen!—and regularly letting them know they're appreciated.

## The Artist at Work

I often tell the story of a hospital that publicized the fact that it planned to add a new wing to its building at a cost of more than $5 million. When the hospital's development officer contacted a wealthy woman who could potentially be the largest donor to the project, she said, "I don't like the design of the wing, and I won't make a donation. It's downright ugly. Please don't call me again."

After that, no one from the development office contacted her—they assumed her mind was made up. At the halfway point of the fundraising campaign, the team wasn't even close to raising the money needed to fund the project.

A member of the team decided to call the woman. He told her he'd like to visit her and get to know her. He asked for an hour of her time, and she grudgingly agreed but said, "If you're coming to talk about that hospital wing, stay right where you are."

During their long talk over tea, the fundraiser didn't mention the hospital project once—he simply showed an interest in her and tried to learn more about her and her philanthropic goals. She began to trust him.

When their conversation ended, he stood up, said goodbye, and started to leave. The woman said, "By the way, that wing they want to put on the hospital is the ugliest thing I've ever seen, but if you change the design, I'll pay for the whole thing." And she did.

The fundraiser didn't visit the woman seeking a simple transaction, a donation for the hospital project; he respected her wishes and put her needs first by taking an interest in her as a person and asking about her goals. After building that all-important trust, she had a perfect opportunity to say what many donors have a need to say: "I want to help."

Sometimes fundraisers forget that donors not only want to help but need to help. If we ask the right questions—and *listen*—we can help our donors achieve their own goals as well as the institution's.

## Creativity and Assertiveness in Action

Nick Scully is one of the most creative major gift fundraisers I've ever met. He always seems to find a way to make things happen. While we worked together on a campaign for Jackson Academy in Jackson, Mississippi, there was one potential prospect we were having trouble getting to see. The prospect always seemed to dodge our efforts to sit down with him. We couldn't find him at home or at his office. He was a very busy guy, and that posed a real challenge.

When faced with this situation—which, by the way, is common in fundraising—we reached out to many people who knew the prospect to find a connection that might help us get his or his wife's attention. During one of those conversations, Nick learned that the wife's uncle had a donut shop in Memphis, Tennessee, and she loved his blueberry donuts.

Well, Nick just happened to live in Memphis. So the next time he headed down to Jackson, he stopped by the donut shop and bought a dozen blueberry donuts. Upon arriving in Jackson, he went to the prospect's home and knocked on the door.

When the wife answered, Nick announced that he was there representing Jackson Academy and he brought her a gift—her uncle's blueberry donuts. She invited him to share the treats, and that visit resulted in a conversation about the future of Jackson Academy and how the couple could help the school achieve its goals.

Ultimately, Jackson Academy secured a six-figure commitment, and Nick proudly earned the moniker Nicky Bag o' Donuts.

While these stories reflect extraordinary instances of generosity, it was the artistry of the fundraisers that created the opportunities.

Without the science of fundraising, however, these fundraisers might not have known who could make a transformational difference for their organization.

## The Science

---

*Science = A systematically organized body of knowledge on a particular subject*
*—Oxford English Dictionary*

---

I have yet to discover an organization that has mastered the "science" of fundraising. To me, mastering this approach to the business means not only having the necessary functions, processes, and data in place but also an appreciation across the organization for the value that the science brings.

Organizations that are serious about the science of fundraising usually have a few things in common. They have at least one staff member dedicated to the functions that comprise the science; they're committed to developing plans and strategies; they prioritize data gathering and have business rules guiding the process; and they have a highly functional database that contains high-quality data and allows staff to easily capture and access that information.

*The greatest value comes from gathering data about our work and using it to do better.*

Many processes in fundraising are a big part of the science of the work, including planning, prospecting, pipeline development, prospect research, strategy development, and donation calculations.

While these functions are critical to fundraising, the greatest scientific value comes from gathering data about our work and using it to do better.

This can take on many forms, so let's start with some basics. At a minimum, a competent fundraiser should be able to answer these questions:

- » How many prospects are needed?

- » How many prospects have been identified?

- » How much philanthropic potential do those prospects represent?

- » How many prospects have been solicited?

- » How many of those prospects made a commitment?

» What percentage of the goal has been achieved?

» What percentage of prospects who were solicited made a commitment?

» For those prospects who made a commitment, what percentage of philanthropic potential has been achieved?

» What is the budget?

» What is the cost per dollar raised, and what is the return on investment?

The answers to these questions give valuable insights into opportunities and challenges that influence progress, highlight the ability to identify and qualify prospects, and provide a way to evaluate outcomes compared to investment of resources. They should also lead to a series of follow-up questions that, when addressed, can help position an organization for greater success. These questions include the following:

» Do we have enough prospects to reach our goal?

» Are people giving more than we anticipated or less?

» Are our solicitation strategies sound, or do they need adjustment?

» Do we need more training?

» Do we need to spend more time engaging and cultivating?

» Should we set our sights higher or lower?

» Are we on track for success?

Beyond the basics, there are endless data points that can be tracked and measured in fundraising.

# Setting Some Rules

*"Heck, even rocket science isn't rocket science."*
*—Joe Allen, physicist and astronaut*

Not too long ago, a director of development for a Compass client came to me and said she had developed a slide deck that detailed more than twenty-five data points for tracking major gift fundraising activity. My first reaction was "Don't ever hand that to a major gift officer, or their head will explode!"

But as we reviewed the slides, I saw the true value of the information, and it led me to develop these basic rules about the science of fundraising:

» Processes, functions, and data analysis are critical to excellence.

» Make data tracking a standard part of business operations.

» Tailor the science to the ability to act on the data.

» Don't try to track everything—tracking even five data points can provide valuable and actionable information.

» Don't select data points if you aren't able to gather information consistently and accurately—inconsistent or inaccurate data isn't useful.

» If you aren't going to report or act on the data, don't track it.

» Be willing to add to or adjust tracked data points to expand fundraising knowledge and impact—there's always something new to be learned.

## A Perfect Balance

I've been privileged to see the art and science of fundraising come into perfect balance on more than one occasion. In those moments, I'm awed by the power of philanthropy.

Years ago, I worked with the University of Minnesota on a very large campaign. A main priority of the initiative was building a new art museum on the banks of the Mississippi, to be designed by legendary architect Frank Gehry. A committee, headed by Penny Winton, was formed to make it happen.

We began looking at prospective donors and working with the committee to help us raise the money. One of our volunteers was Billy Weisman, a local entrepreneur and an alumnus of "the U."

The campaign started slowly, but the committee was determined to bring the new art museum to life. One day Billy came to us with a story. On a Sunday morning, he got a phone call at home from a man named Fred Weisman. Fred's father, whose name was William Weisman, was from Minneapolis. Fred wanted to know if he and Billy were related.

"I have a private jet at the airport," Fred said to Billy on the call. "Come and visit. I'd like to meet you." Billy was taken aback, and he didn't think they were related, so he declined the offer.

After he hung up the phone and told his wife about the call, she said, "Are you crazy? He's got his own jet. Let's go meet him."

So they did. Although the two men learned they weren't related, they struck up a friendship and met often. During that time, Billy learned of Fred's philanthropy and his interest in art—he started the Weisman Art Foundation—and Billy thought he might be interested in contributing to the new art museum.

He shared this opportunity with the university's development staff, and they went to work. Through research, they discovered that Fred was a student at the U during the Great Depression, but he couldn't afford to complete his degree. They learned about Fred's dad, William, who had achieved business success in Minneapolis and was very philanthropic.

During their research, they discovered a historic photograph of the William Weisman building in Minneapolis (which had long since been torn down). They enlarged that photo and put it in an attractive frame, and Billy presented it to Fred as a gift.

That act touched Fred deeply. He had never seen the photo and didn't know it existed. He was more than impressed by the effort to connect with him on a personal level, and as a result, his relationship with the U and Billy flourished. When the moment was right, the fundraising team asked Fred to be the lead patron of the new art museum.

He said yes, and today the museum bears his name: The Frederick R. Weisman Art Museum.

This is a great example of how the art and science of fundraising came together perfectly and created a magic moment for both the donor and the institution ... a moment that led to great things.

## Finding Balance

In their efforts to achieve an organization's goals, the fundraising team must create a form of alchemy, blending the science of fundraising, which is based on tried-and-true processes, and the art, which brings creativity and empathy into play. Successfully combining these two elements can produce remarkable results.

I'll be the first to admit that, as a fundraiser, I was more an artist than a scientist. There were times when I felt myself bumping against the science in ways that would limit my creativity. Today I see the incredible value of both, and I seek opportunities to share that perspective.

Doing the science—asking the right questions, measuring the things that can be acted upon, collecting accurate data, analyzing it, and using it well—positions organizations to be effective at the art of fundraising.

As fundraisers strive to balance the art and the science during a campaign, they must remember to keep the organization's main, enduring guiding light—its mission—in clear view.

"Outstanding [organizations] have one thing in common: an absolute sense of mission."

—ZIG ZIGLAR, SECRETS OF CLOSING THE SALE

## CHAPTER 3

# MISSION MATTERS

I'd like to tell you a story.

On the South Side of Pittsburgh, at 81 South Nineteenth Street, there's a large, stately church in a quiet residential and commercial neighborhood. The church is well taken care of, but it's not used as a church anymore.

When you go inside and look around, you see offices, meeting spaces, and a large gathering place in what used to be the sanctuary. If you look up, there's a balcony along the walls, winding all the way around the church. On the balcony are ten small houses.

Each house has a door, a window with a flower box, a skylight, and a roof with a chimney. In the houses, meeting places, and quiet spaces in the building, life-changing things happen.

It's where the work of PAAR—Pittsburgh Action Against Rape— takes place every day.

## Limited Resources

When I first met the people of PAAR, their offices were in the Oakland section of Pittsburgh, a neighborhood so dangerous that clients were afraid to visit. The organization had about six thousand clients who were victims of domestic and sexual abuse—50 percent of them were children.

PAAR had very limited financial means and was often mired in the politics and bureaucracy of Pittsburgh. Its resources—and patience—were being stretched to the breaking point. The PAAR staff thought no one in Pittsburgh cared about the amazing work they did to help survivors put their lives back together.

The PAAR team knew they needed a new location, one that matched who they were—welcoming, caring, and supportive.

Two courageous leaders of PAAR—Molly Knox and Pat Hargest—had a vision of what the organization could be. They dreamt about providing higher levels of safety, comfort, and healing for their clients. But they didn't have the financial resources to make their dream a reality.

They had to do something. Their clients' needs were too great. They had to make a difference in their clients' lives, and they had to do it right away.

## Taking the First Step

When I heard the story of PAAR at a meeting of their board, I was in awe of the work being done and the vision for the future, and for the first time in my consulting career, I was prompted to ask a client, "How long do you want to be poor?" This question caused a shift in thinking that led to action at PAAR and proved invaluable from that point forward in my discussions with other nonprofits in need.

I was honored to be hired to conduct a planning study that would help create a plan to raise funds that would lift PAAR out of its desperate situation.

During the study, I interviewed Frank Cahouet, CEO of Mellon Bank, who made small donations to PAAR but had never been more involved than that. Frank told me he believed in PAAR and had powerful personal reasons why he wanted to chair the new fundraising campaign.

The study showed positive results—there were a number of funding sources in Pittsburgh that PAAR could approach. Unsure of themselves, the team at PAAR took one tentative step at a time and started their campaign with Frank leading the way.

With the guidance of a steering committee, the campaign moved ahead, and good things happened. PAAR exceeded its fundraising goal by 50 percent. (Other CEOs and foundations in Pittsburgh couldn't say no to Frank.)

## A Fresh Start

PAAR bought the church and renovated it, turning it into an urban oasis where real and lasting healing happens. As anticipated, campaign success benefited PAAR's clients in both measurable and immeasurable ways. But what moves me to this day is a different perspective that Molly shared with me shortly after the campaign ended.

She explained that, because of the campaign, the staff at PAAR learned that Pittsburgh and all of Allegheny County not only knew of them but believed in the work they did. They learned that all their fundraising prospects wanted to support them—every one of them made a gift. They learned that they were respected and valued as an organization. They learned that Pittsburgh cared. They learned that their mission mattered to far more people than they ever imagined.

In the process of conducting the campaign, PAAR strengthened its board, built the capacity to sustain itself over time through philanthropy, became a major player in Pittsburgh and a leader in social service delivery, and established a reputation throughout the region and the state for its expertise in recovery from sexual and domestic violence.

> *They learned that their mission mattered to far more people than they ever imagined.*

These days, I can barely remember where I was yesterday, and I can't seem to find the "Reply All" button in Outlook. But I'll never forget PAAR, Molly Knox, Pat Hargest, and Frank Cahouet. I'll never forget the drawings and the T-shirts that hung on the walls of that church, made by kids who were victims of abuse.

Working with PAAR is the most important fundraising work I've ever done. That organization is a great example of achieving its mission—transforming itself from being needy to being worthy—and for many nonprofit organizations, that transformation is absolutely essential for fundraising success.

*"Imagine if everyone who wanted to change the world knew they could."*

—JAMES GREGORY LORD,
THE RAISING OF MONEY

## CHAPTER 4

# NEEDY VERSUS WORTHY

In terms of fundraising, it's inevitable that nonprofit organizations are perceived in one of two ways: needy or worthy.

## *Needy*

Needy nonprofits always seem to be in crisis, facing financial conditions that threaten to close their doors and end their important work. They're always trying to survive the year, always trying to make ends meet, and they devote whatever resources they can to their programs.

Within those organizations, being under-resourced creates a culture of scarcity. They exist under constant threat and don't have enough of anything. They'd love to hire an experienced director of development to run their fundraising operation, but they can't pay well, so they have an inexperienced staff that has trouble delivering the results they need.

A donor who gives to a nonprofit that is needy will have to do that every year to ensure the long-term value of their investment. Without the structure or resources needed to generate enough funding for sustainability, the organization runs a high, ongoing risk of failure.

I've heard donors say things like this about needy organizations: "I'm going to support them—I like what they do—but I'm never going to give them a big gift because they're always in crisis mode and I'm not sure they'll be around very long." Or: "I don't have the confidence they can handle a large gift."

## Worthy

Worthy organizations, on the other hand, demonstrate fundraising success. They're solid nonprofits that have a vision and a good plan, and they raise more money every year. They know where they're going, and they're always in planning mode, always moving forward.

Why is it that organizations that already have the most money can raise the most money? Because they have a history of raising funds and accomplishing big things, and donors perceive them as worthy of their support.

> **Worthy organizations know where they're going, and they're always in planning mode, always moving forward.**

Donors who consider making a big gift want their dollars to make a difference. They give to organizations that will accomplish goals that donors want to see accomplished. They know that the organizations will be around for a long time, and they invest in their future.

To ensure sustainability, needy organizations must become worthy organizations—this transformation leads to increased philanthropy.

# Transformation

As a consultant, I've been fortunate to aid many clients on this journey of transformation. It can be a long process, but it's well worth the effort.

The National Park Trust ("the Park Trust") demonstrated this. That organization's mission is to help national parks thrive in the United States by buying private lands and donating them to the parks. They run terrific educational programs—like the Buddy Bison program, which connects kids with parks across the country—that teach kids about national parks and how to steward them and protect the environment.

I met with the executive director of the Park Trust, Grace Lee, when our company provided pro bono consulting services to the National Park Service. Grace is a skilled and energetic leader, but back then, the organization operated on a meager budget and needed help raising funds.

Grace had a core group of board members who strongly believed in the Park Trust, its work, and its leadership. The organization had great programs and a big name, but a small budget.

During a conversation with Grace and her board, I once again asked that important question: "How long do you want to be poor?"

They identified several ways they could strengthen their position:

» Enlist more board members who could partner with staff and attract more funds.

» Strengthen and increase the number of educational programs that helped kids around the country become more involved with the parks and nature.

» Adopt a change in attitude and action from a culture of scarcity to a culture of philanthropy.

Working as a team, Grace and the board made all those changes. As a result, the Park Trust increased its ability to raise more money each year.

Their progress with fundraising allowed them to dream bigger, provide more programs, and attract more people to their board who could make a difference. Grace and her team transformed the organization from needy to worthy, and the increased support they received—locally and nationally—showed that people saw them as a thriving, successful organization that deserved their gifts.

# The Journey

---

*"The only impossible journey is the one you never begin."*

*—Tony Robbins*

---

The journey from needy to worthy requires these things:

**Vision.** Everything starts with a vision that says

- » this is who we are,

- » this is what we do,

- » this is why we do it,

- » this is where we're going, and

- » this is what we will be ten years from today.

**Goals.** An organization must identify its goals and the impact that attaining them will have.

**Plan.** An effective plan outlines how an organization will accomplish its goals and how long it will take to get there.

**Budget.** It's important to know the number and types of resources in terms of personnel, programs, and dollars needed to accomplish the plan.

**Programs.** Be sure that programs are worthy of investment—high-quality programs inspire donors and drive participation.

**Champions.** The board of directors must champion the organization and passionately lead the way in messaging, engagement, and philanthropy.

**Attitude.** The fundraising team must act like it's worthy, demonstrate that it's worthy, stop apologizing for why it can't do things, and start talking about opportunities and what is possible with more investment.

Completing the journey from needy to worthy can be a main part of an organization's vision for the future. Fundraisers must refer to the vision consistently—it serves as an essential, aspirational template for their day-to-day work.

"A vision is not just a picture of what could be; it is an appeal to our better selves, a call to become something more."

—ROSABETH MOSS KANTER, HARVARD BUSINESS SCHOOL

CHAPTER 5

# IT ALL STARTS WITH A VISION

A clearly defined vision is essential for fundraising success. A vision for what an organization wants to achieve—actually, what it wants to be—will affect every aspect of a campaign, from setting fundraising goals to creating a positive image among constituents.

What exactly is a vision? It's a dream. It's an audacious idea. It's comprised of great aspirations. It articulates answers to many questions: If money were no object, what could we do? What would we do? What would we be? How would we help those we serve? And how might we help make the world a better place?

Though a well-conceived vision can easily be communicated to those inside and outside of an organization, it can take years to become a reality.

# Where Do You Want to Go?

---

*"If you don't know where you're going, any road will take you there."*

—Lewis Carroll

---

I can't overemphasize the importance of vision to fundraising. Even organizations that are successful in fulfilling their mission must have a vision to sustain the work they do.

I've seen how a lack of vision impedes an organization because the people who work there, those who donate there, and those who volunteer there all want the answer to one question: Where are we going?

Standing still—without an inspiring vision for the future—is deadly for any nonprofit, and in the competition for philanthropic funds, organizations without a vision will lose out every time to those that are ambitious and forward-thinking.

Over the course of my career, I've met visionary leaders who can easily articulate where they want their organization to go and what they want it to become. I've worked with complex institutions where the vision is derived from a well-conceived strategic plan that assesses the organization's strengths, weaknesses, opportunities, and threats and states objectives that will advance it to the next level.

But for many organizations, formulating a vision can be very challenging.

Years ago, I met with the president of a prestigious college who told me she wanted to raise $200 million. I asked her, "What's your vision for this college? What do you want it to be?"

She said, "We want to be better."

I said, "OK, great. Do you want a better curriculum, better faculty, better facilities, better financial endowment, better students? How do you want to be better?"

"I don't know," she said. "Go talk to the dean."

So I headed off to the dean's office and asked him the same question.

He looked at me, then turned to the bookcase behind him. He reached up and grabbed a dusty document and said, "We did this plan three years ago."

I said, "That's great. What does it say?"

"I don't know. I never read it. Besides, isn't that what we hired you for?"

Summoning up all the patience I could muster, I told him, "If you want my help, let's get the school's administrators and board of directors together to sit down and talk with each other and decide what you want to do. That will help you determine your vision—your dreams for this institution.

"If you don't have a vision, you shouldn't be out there trying to raise money. You're not going to be successful because people are going to ask, 'Why are you doing this? Why are you asking me for money?' And you won't have a good answer."

Evidently, the college administration and the board didn't want to make the effort—they never went forward with a campaign.

# Building a Shared Vision— SOARing with Your Board

*"I don't skate to where the puck is; I skate to where it's going to be."*

—Wayne Gretzky

If a nonprofit leader struggles to answer "If money were no object, tell me what this organization can do, what it can be, and where you want it to go," it's important to take a step back and help that person develop a vision for the future.

To aid organizations with this, I've relied on a variety of tactics over the years. I've found, however, that traditional strategic planning methods and SWOT (Strengths, Weaknesses, Opportunities, and Threats) analyses tend to get mired in tactics and execution, and they focus on weaknesses.

> **If money were no object, tell me what this organization can do, what it can be, and where you want it to go.**

To effectively engage board members in the planning process and ensure their time is used productively, we need to take a broader view of the organization and its aspirations. When I searched for a process that was more uplifting and aspirational—a positive, engaging experience that unites board members and staff leaders in a shared vision—I discovered SOAR (Strengths, Opportunities, Aspirations, and Results).

Created by Jacqueline Stavros and Gina Hinrichs, SOAR is designed to help an organization craft a shared vision—a "big idea" for the future.

Here's how Compass implements SOAR in small group workshops:

### S (Strengths). What are you good at?

In a retreat format for board members and staff leadership, small groups identify, record, and report the organization's strengths for planning purposes. The energetic discussions set a positive tone for creating a vision.

### O (Opportunities). Based on what you're good at, what opportunities are out there?

After listing strengths in the first step, the group zeroes in on potential opportunities. Participants working in small groups are encouraged to think outside the box as they align opportunities with strengths. Ideas are then shared with the entire group.

### A (Aspirations). Based on your strengths and opportunities, what are the big ideas for your future?

The team moves on to think about "big ideas" that will be transformational, impacting the future path of the organization. This part of the process—active discussion and sharing ideas that people are passionate about—is exciting for the entire group. The goal is to establish two or three ideas that will be the foundation for future discussions about vision.

### R (Results). What will you need to make the big idea a reality?

For the last step of the SOAR process, the group is asked to create a mental picture of what success would look like. The question guiding the discussion is "If we do our work according to the ideas we generated in SOAR, what will our organization be?" The group defines the new vision and details what they must do to achieve it.

Through SOAR, the board and leadership staff are part of a decision-making process that unites them, helps them focus on the core values and priorities of the organization, establishes benchmarks for success, and inspires them to action.

This collaboration is essential. Often, when a leader establishes an organization's vision without input from their team, the team must be regularly reminded of what the vision is. But when the entire group contributes to the vision, no one has to be reminded of it—they helped to create it, they know very well what it is, and they will work hard to make it a reality.

## From Vision to Reality

---

*"Chase the vision, not the money. The money will end up following you."*

—Tony Hsieh, CEO, Zappos

---

Henri Landwirth—Holocaust survivor, hotelier, and philanthropist—had a wonderful vision, and through years of hard work and near-obsessive focus, it became a reality. It became Give Kids the World. The nonprofit in Kissimmee, Florida, provides festive, weeklong, cost-free vacations for families from around the world with children who have life-threatening illnesses.

Back in the 1980s, Henri didn't seem like someone who would dedicate his life to creating magical experiences for children—he was the manager of a Holiday Inn near Brevard County, Florida, home of Cape Canaveral, where many US spacecraft were launched.

Henri was introduced to a little girl named Amy who was dying of leukemia. One of her fondest wishes was to go to Walt Disney World Resort and enjoy the magical theme parks. Henri was moved by Amy's situation and promised to get tickets to Disney World for her and her family. He offered to let them stay at his Holiday Inn for one week, free of charge.

Although Henri worked day and night to arrange the vacation, before his plans were complete, time ran out—Amy passed away.

Henri was heartbroken. He vowed that no child in the same situation would ever be failed again. Initially, he had no idea how to make good on his vow, but as he shared Amy's story and his own passion to help, a vision for Give Kids the World emerged.

Henri enlisted the support of colleagues in the hospitality and tourism industries to help him bring special families to Florida in a timely manner.

As the number of families asking for vacations grew, it was clear he needed a venue that could fulfill all their needs. In 1989, Give Kids the World Village opened, and Henri's vision became a thirty-one-acre reality.

Today, the Village is an eighty-nine-acre resort with 166 villa accommodations, entertainment attractions, and activities for children of all ages and abilities.

Families who come to Give Kids the World stay for one week in a suite that is designed especially for them. Meals are prepared to serve children's dietary needs, and the organization gives tickets and transportation to Disney World, Universal Studios, SeaWorld, and other attractions.

Today, led by Pam Landwirth, Give Kids the World has welcomed more than 176,000 families from all fifty states and seventy-six countries, and it's one of the largest volunteer organizations in the world.

Henri Landwirth's vision launched Give Kids the World, and he made it happen through relentless desire, compassion, and determination.

*"I often tell people I live on borrowed time—and for today, my goal is to give something to someone in need, to reach out to someone who needs a hand. For today, I will try to be a better man."*
*—Henri Landwirth*

Just as Landwirth's blend of admirable personality traits helped him achieve great success, a fundraising campaign must have a blend of four elements, working in harmony, to reach its ambitious goals.

*"The secret of success
is to do common things
uncommonly well."*

—JOHN D. ROCKEFELLER

CHAPTER 6

# THE SECRET SAUCE

I've been a fundraising consultant for many years, and I hear one question all the time: "What's the secret to a successful fundraising campaign?"

I answer that there are no guarantees—many factors affect a campaign, both positively and negatively—but I know the "secret sauce" that can make any campaign a winner in serving a worthy organization.

To achieve campaign success, an organization must have these four elements—I call them the "predictive indicators for success"—and the elements must work together in harmony:

## *A good reason for raising money.*

It's essential that, in its appeal for funds, a nonprofit makes a compelling case for support. Every organization has its own story, and potential donors need to hear about its history, growth, impact on the people it serves, vision for the future, and value to the community.

The story must say, "This is who we are, and this is what we do. Here's why we do it, and here are the reasons we're good at it. We address these needs, and we'll continue to do that in the future … with your help."

There's a lot of competition for support. To be successful an organization must make it easy for prospective donors to say yes. The case for support must be compelling, urgent, unique, and worthy. Donors have a need to give, so it is important to show how their gift will make a difference.

### Enough philanthropic potential to reach the goal.

The success of a campaign depends on securing donations of specified amounts that add up to the goal.

Prospects are individuals, corporations, and foundations that have an interest in a nonprofit organization's work. They give in proportion to their ability to give, the size of the goal, and the gifts of others.

Determining the potential within a constituency may require several steps, including reviewing current prospect and donor lists, conducting confidential interviews during a planning or feasibility study, or implementing a wealth screening.

These steps help answer a series of critical questions about campaign potential: Are there enough prospects—if they respond to the campaign—to make it successful? Will those prospects provide the number and sizes of gifts necessary? How well do we know those prospects? How can we help our prospects understand the worthiness of our vision and the importance of their contributions? The answers to these questions become the foundation of a campaign strategy.

## *Volunteer leadership that is willing to ask for gifts.*

The best volunteers set the philanthropic tone and provide access to people who can invest in an organization.

They make an effort to understand and internalize the case for support; they prioritize the work they do on behalf of a campaign; they give access to their personal network and relationships; they make a gift that is a true reflection of their ability and interest; and—most important— they are there to solicit a gift when the time is right.

> *Finding the right volunteers can be challenging, but it's worth the effort. They're the key to maximizing donations.*

Finding the right volunteers can be challenging, but it's worth the effort. They're the key to maximizing donations within a constituency.

## *Resources to strategically support a campaign.*

Conducting a campaign isn't "business as usual." A campaign, by definition, has a significant fundraising goal that must be met within a defined timeframe, that will support urgent objectives, and that will help the organization realize its vision. To this end, organizations must have the resources to create an environment for campaign success.

Every organization is different, and resources may be needed to help with identifying prospects, creating communications, conducting events, funding travel for prospect visits, supporting volunteers, personalizing donor stewardship, upgrading tracking and reporting systems, hiring campaign-specific staff, and, most importantly, engaging external expertise to ensure flawless campaign execution.

If an organization can establish these four elements to support a campaign, the road to success is wide open. However, evaluating each of these elements when preparing for a campaign isn't always easy. Nonprofit executives and governing boards can save themselves a lot of time and stress if they conduct a readiness assessment before a campaign to find out if these predictive indicators for success are in place.

If they are, the fundraising team can move full speed ahead with their campaign. Next, they need to determine how they will communicate their mission to prospective donors and volunteers to bring them onboard. Like a good lawyer representing a client, the team must create a compelling case.

"We are all storytellers. We all live in a network of stories. There isn't a stronger connection between people than storytelling."

—JIMMY NEIL SMITH, FOUNDER, INTERNATIONAL STORYTELLING CENTER

# CHAPTER 7

# A CASE TO REMEMBER

I believe every organization has a story to tell—a story of how it was born, what it does, the impact it has on society, the values it represents, and, most of all, its dreams for the future. This story must be told with emotion and impact because it's about real people, real problems, and real solutions.

I'm always excited to hear how an organization talks about itself. While every nonprofit faces challenges, most have wondrous ideas, plans, and goals, all focused on strengthening their ability to make the world a better place.

Translating all that into a memorable case for support is the first step in making those dreams come true.

# Capture Hearts and Minds

---

*"To reach your own goals and dreams, you must first learn how to assist others in reaching theirs."*

—Joe Gibbs

---

While a vision can spark emotions that prompt philanthropic support, organizations that can translate that vision into a plan can capture the hearts *and* minds of prospects and donors.

The case for support for Youth for Tomorrow, founded by Super Bowl–winning coach and NASCAR team owner Joe Gibbs, does just that. Troubled by what he witnessed while working with at-risk adolescents in Washington, DC, during his time coaching the Washington Redskins, Joe developed a vision for helping boys and girls. That vision was translated into a plan that included character rehabilitation, quality education, personal faith, and life-skill development.

The result was a powerful story that captured the hearts and minds of many friends, business contacts, and, of course, Redskins fans. Youth for Tomorrow opened its doors in 1986, and the organization thrives to this day under the leadership of Dr. Gary Jones who, inspired by Joe's vision and his own commitment to helping young people, continues to expand the story with new chapters of success and growth.

Because of Jones's unwavering commitment and incessant fundraising, Youth for Tomorrow is now an organization that offers sixteen nationally accredited programs and serves more than eight thousand children and adults every year. The Youth for Tomorrow two-hundred-acre main campus in Bristow, Virginia, includes eleven residential facilities, a forty-thousand-square-foot school, and a 335-seat chapel.

Joe, a strong Christian, will tell you something that reveals a lot about him. He says that on the day he goes to meet his Maker, the Lord isn't going to congratulate him on his Super Bowl championships or NASCAR wins. He's going to tell the story of Youth for Tomorrow and the healing things the organization does for children. Joe says it's one of the things that gives his life meaning and purpose.

# Crafting a Case

Most nonprofits underestimate how difficult it can be to create a compelling case for support, but for those that are intentional about it, it can be a positive growth experience.

Here are important things to consider when crafting an organization's case:

## What is the story?

An organization must tell people its story. When and why did it start? How did it get to where it is? What has been accomplished, and what will be accomplished in the future? People want to know that it's a valued organization that makes a difference.

## What is the vision?

The organization must be clear about what it's striving to become. The vision can be aspirational but must describe specific goals and how they were determined. The case must be the result of a planning process that has defined goals and objectives that are embraced by all parts of the organization.

## What societal issues is the organization solving?

The case must be bigger than the organization—it must affect society in a way that is easily understood by your constituency. It's important to explain how the organization will make an impact on a problem and focus on opportunities more than needs. If the issue is homelessness in America, speak to the enormity of the problem nationally and how the organization will make a difference in its region.

> *The case must be bigger than the organization—it must affect society in a way that is easily understood.*

## Why is the organization the best one to address these issues?

Most likely, the organization isn't the only one in the field, but its specific background, history, and constituencies uniquely position it for impact. It's important to draw on those things to set the organization apart and convey that uniqueness throughout the case.

## How are the goals going to be accomplished?

The fundraising team must tell the story of the organization by clearly describing its programs. Words and numbers can be intertwined to fully demonstrate the organization's impact. Describe the plan that was created to achieve the vision and the investment it will take to make it happen. Let people in on the plan, and give them an opportunity to identify with it and be part of the team.

### What is the impact on constituents?

Describe ideal outcomes. In objective terms, show how the organization will measure success.

The organization must demonstrate that it always does what it promises to do. Donors want to know that their investments will make a difference and the organization knows what success looks like.

### What are donors being asked to do?

An effective case includes a clear fundraising goal and a call to action so prospective donors know what the fundraising team is asking of them. Be direct and be bold—don't be afraid to ask for their help.

In developing the case for support—in addition to presenting big ideas—include data that will be helpful for prospective donors. The case isn't a data-driven document, but it's important to include data for those who like to see the numbers.

## Connect, Engage, Inspire

To create a case that connects, engages, and inspires its audience, make it …

**Brief.** Replace lengthy paragraphs with meaningful infographics, photographs, or other imagery that tell the story in a more concise, visual way.

**Forward-thinking.** Include accomplishments that add legitimacy to the organization's programs, but do so quickly, then shift to forward-thinking narrative.

**Optimistic.** Philanthropy flourishes in an atmosphere of optimism. Express confidence in the organization's ability to achieve its goals.

**Big picture.** Effective fundraisers don't talk much about hospitals, emergency rooms, or clinics; they tell a story about improving health. They don't talk about schools, colleges, endowments, and buildings; they tell a story about a student thriving because of a quality education.

**Authentic.** It's important to sincerely express that because of the good things the organization does, it's respected, and the world is a better place.

A well-crafted case for support will be complex, and while there are many tools for presenting it—a printed document that shows the goals of the campaign, a video that uses people and places to deliver the message, a website that highlights campaign impact, or direct mail efforts that share information with a broad constituency—the most effective tools are the face-to-face conversations that staff, board, and volunteers have with prospects and donors.

## Messaging the Case

---

*"One story beats a dozen adjectives. Don't use adjectives. Use stories."*

—*Harry Beckwith,* Selling the Invisible

---

Staff and volunteers will be ambassadors for an organization's campaign. They often find it difficult, however, to communicate the case for support. Some feel they have to memorize it to get it right or that they must be experts on all elements of the case so they can answer any question that arises.

For some, the thought of sharing the message with others can be intimidating, as they struggle to find the right words and say them well. They want to represent the organization in a way that will drive success.

The key to presenting the case comfortably and naturally is to *make it personal.* I encourage staff and volunteers to put down their notes and …

> » Tell their story. Explain why the organization is so important to you that you give it your time, expertise, and resources.

> » Be authentic. Speak your truth. If you're asked a question and you don't know the answer, tell them that you don't know but you'll find the answer and get back to them quickly. Stick to talking about what you know and what you believe.

> » Speak from the heart. Be willing to share your emotional connection to the organization. Tell your own story in your own voice.

No case for support is as powerful as someone who delivers it in their own words and from the heart.

At a board meeting of an independent school in Maryland, I promoted this approach. "Tell your story," I said. "Tell me why you're here, why this school is important to you and your family, and why you care so much." We went around the room, and everyone told their story. There were emotions, passion, dedication, heartbreak, and dreams for the school and the children. There were tears and hugs and insights.

The session was powerful and magical. People learned from each other's experience and passion—and found ways to deliver the message in a personal and persuasive way.

When the case for a campaign is presented this way, it's hard for a prospect to say no. While they may disagree with the plan and objectives, they can't say that it's not important to you. When the conversation begins on a powerful and personal note, the transition to asking for money is easier as well. "Will you join me?" is a powerful question—but not an intimidating one—when presented in the context of how much you care.

## Practice Makes Perfect

Making it personal can be risky. Often, both staff and volunteers are anxious about revealing their personal feelings about an organization, so we prepare through ...

> » Training. Everybody gets better with practice. We don't ask them to create an elevator speech; we ask them to have a conversation about the organization and its efforts—in their own words.

> » Role play. Practicing out loud in front of others helps people become comfortable with their words and the situation.

I remember a college that used an actor, along with the president of the school, to create a multimedia presentation of its case for support. The actor did the first take perfectly. The president needed eighty-eight takes, and we finally spliced together segments of each take to create an appropriate message and image. Not everyone comes to this easily.

# What We Leave Behind

In finding ways to make communicating the case easier, it's important to understand that while most donors make emotional decisions about giving, they rely on the materials they receive to rationalize those decisions.

It's important to give staff and volunteers materials they can leave behind for a prospect to review as they consider making a donation. These materials can be in many forms, but they should reiterate the most important aspects of the case.

One of the most creative "leave-behinds" I've seen was produced by the Wyoming chapter of the Nature Conservancy. The staff created a printed placemat and placed it in front of everyone in meetings as they explained their love for and commitment to Wyoming. The placemat served as a printed "dashboard" of the principles and priorities of the chapter's vision for conservation. It became an effective tool for conversation and a persuasive reminder for the donor.

Even with a solid case for support, some fundraisers struggle to determine where the money will come from. Who will their donors be? How many donors will they need to reach a lofty goal? Read on to learn how a gifts chart can be a valuable tool for figuring it all out.

"Have a bias towards action—
let's see something happen
now. You can break that big
plan into small steps and take
the first step right away."

—INDIRA GANDHI

CHAPTER 8

# THE MIGHTY GIFTS CHART

Identifying the potential for any fundraising initiative is important, but an organization doesn't need to know exactly where every dollar will come from before kicking off an ambitious campaign. However, progress in relation to the goal must be accurately tracked every step of the way. To do this, I rely on a gifts chart.

For every gifts chart I've created in my career, however, I have also heard a fundraiser disregard its importance and value to their efforts. I believe this is based on a failure to understand how to effectively use the critical information that a carefully developed gifts chart provides.

Here's how I harness the power of the gifts chart.

## Creating a Gifts Chart

A gifts chart can be created for any organization, but one size doesn't fit all. Gifts charts vary based on the size and duration of a campaign and even the subsector served by the nonprofit. Billion-dollar gifts charts look different than $10 million gifts charts, higher education gifts charts look different than social service gifts charts, and annual fund gifts charts look different than capital campaign gifts charts.

For a campaign in which multiyear commitments will be solicited in a timeframe that allows plenty of opportunity for identifying, qualifying, and cultivating new prospects, a gifts chart will be aspirational—reflecting the size and number of commitments needed based on an ideal model that breaks down the goal by percentage:

» Top Gift—20%–25% of Goal

» Top-Ten Gifts—50%–60% of Goal

» Remaining Gifts—40%–50% of Goal

For an annual campaign in which the timeframe for building a pipeline of new donors is much shorter, the gifts chart focuses on current and recent donors who have high potential to repeat or increase their annual giving and prospects who were recently cultivated for the current year.

## Winning the Campaign on Paper

At an organization I was counseling, I saw a young corporate gift officer who was visibly upset. She was in her office in tears. I wanted to help, and I asked her what was wrong.

"I have a million-dollar goal this year," she said, "but as hard as I try, I can't figure out how to get there." This was a big campaign for her, and she wanted very much to be successful.

"I've been where you are," I said, "so let's see if we can figure it out together. If we want to be successful in getting to goal, first we have to *win the campaign on paper.*"

"Meaning what?" she asked.

"From my experience, to be successful, it will take about three prospects for each gift you need," I said.

"Why three?" she asked.

"Over the years, I've learned that one of those prospects will say no or make only a token gift; one will make a gift, but not nearly the amount they were asked to give; and one will give what you asked for, or reasonably close," I explained. "Your organization represents a worthy cause, and it has a well-established culture of philanthropy. You cultivated your donors,

> *If we want to be successful in getting to goal, first we have to win the campaign on paper.*

and they understand the need for philanthropic support, so the three-to-one ratio might just work. If this was a new organization or an organization that didn't have a culture of philanthropy, we might need more than three-to-one."

"How do I figure this out?" she asked.

"Let's look at how many prospects you have who gave last year—and the amount they gave—and how many of them are likely to repeat their support," I said. "Let's also consider how many of them might not support you this year and how many might be able to consider increasing their support. Let's make a list of these things."

After we made the list, I said, "Now, we need to compare the list with a gifts chart for $1 million."

"How do you do that?" she asked. So I walked her through the process of developing a gifts chart specifically for her organization and prospect portfolio. This is what we came up with:

| GIFTS CHART~ OBJECTIVE: $1,000,000 | | | | |
|---|---|---|---|---|
| **GIFTS NEEDED** | **AMOUNT** | **TOTAL** | **CUMULATIVE TOTAL** | **% OF OBJECTIVE** |
| 1 | $200,000 | $200,000 | $200,000 | 20% |
| 2 | $100,000 | $200,000 | $400,000 | |
| 3 | $50,000 | $150,000 | $550,000 | |
| 4 | $25,000 | $100,000 | $650,000 | 65% |
| 10 | $10,000 | $100,000 | $750,000 | |
| 15 | $5,000 | $75,000 | $825,000 | |
| 30 | $2,500 | $75,000 | $900,000 | |
| 50 | $1,000 | $50,000 | $950,000 | 95% |
| many | below $10,000 | $50,000 | $1,000,000 | 100% |

According to the chart, she needed 115 gifts of $1,000 or more. After applying a three-to-one ratio, we calculated she needed 345 total prospects to be successful.

"What's next?" she asked.

"Take the list we created, and align each name with the donation you're projecting they will make this year," I instructed.

After that, we looked at past donors to see if any could be brought back, and we aligned them with the chart as well. When we finished, we were able to identify the gaps in philanthropic potential. It turned out that she needed forty-five new prospects that year to make her goal.

Now she knew what she needed to do to be successful, and that took a huge weight from her shoulders. For her, it was an epiphany. She could now see where she needed to invest her time and effort, and she went on to have an over-the-goal successful campaign.

## The Trickle-Down Effect

While I push my clients to identify at least three different prospects for every gift on a gifts chart, I recognize that, as gifts are secured, prospects who don't give at the level projected will likely "trickle down," making commitments at a lower level.

While this would imply that a ratio of less than three-to-one may be appropriate for some of the lower gift levels, I don't recommend making those adjustments. I believe the trickle-down effect serves as a built-in safety net and having more prospects than necessary at any giving level will better position your organization for success.

## A Road Map for Success

Beyond identifying gaps in philanthropic potential, I believe a gifts chart is the starting point for planning any fundraising effort.

A gifts chart provides a road map for success by aligning every aspect of a campaign to the activities that will have the greatest impact: identification, qualification, cultivation, solicitation, and stewardship of prospects.

A gifts chart informs planning and execution by clarifying the number and sizes of gifts needed to reach campaign goals; the number of prospects needed to obtain those gifts; the resources and manpower necessary to efficiently move prospects through the fundraising cycle; and the goals, timelines, and deadlines to keep the campaign on course.

For organizations with greater gaps in philanthropic potential—those in the early stages of developing a robust pipeline of prospects—the campaign timeline will be extended, the resources invested in prospect research will be increased, and a broad communications strategy will be implemented.

For organizations with sophisticated fundraising programs, investments in gift officers and volunteer support to manage prospect portfolios are a priority.

Activating the gifts chart as a planning tool will also engender the confidence of the board and volunteers. Connecting strategies, timelines, and resources to the prospect potential on a gifts chart is reassuring as the team pursues ambitious goals. The gifts chart establishes campaign phases and accountability for implementation.

The gifts chart clearly reveals the magnitude of the project and the seemingly endless list of tasks to be done. The only way to reach the finish line on time is by recruiting, training, and supporting a capable and versatile team.

"The good Lord must have loved ordinary people, because He made so many of us—and every day, ordinary people do extraordinary things."

—JIM VALVANO,
NATIONAL CHAMPION COLLEGE
BASKETBALL COACH

CHAPTER 9

# BUILDING A TEAM

The importance of building a team to implement a fundraising campaign can't be overemphasized. This team must include dedicated leadership and staff and a corps of committed volunteers.

In addition to providing the basic manpower needed to manage a large number of prospects, volunteers bring credibility, set an example with their own giving, raise the sights of others, and provide access to sources of philanthropy that may otherwise be unreachable.

I've been fortunate to work with exceptional boards and volunteers. I've seen those people come together and accomplish extraordinary things.

The power of volunteerism changed everything for Wilson College, where I was privileged to serve as resident counsel for their first "real" fundraising campaign.

## The Wilson Women

In 1869, Sarah Wilson provided the funding for Wilson College in Chambersburg, Pennsylvania. She was the first living woman to endow an institution of higher education for women, and the college bears her name.

She wanted the college to "spend time in development of thought so that pupils will learn to think for themselves, and thus become leaders, instead of followers, in society."

The college became famous in March 1979 when, in response to poor economic conditions, its board voted to close the school, sell the campus, and create an educational foundation that supported women. In response, Wilson alumnae sued the board, hoping to reverse the decision.

The day before the school's final commencement ceremony, the court sided with the alumnae and overturned the decision to close the college. (This precedent-setting decision still serves as a strong, unique case study for liberal arts colleges.)

Energized by the decision, an army of "Wilson Women" volunteered to come to campus, get students and faculty back, refurbish campus facilities, staff the college where needed, and quickly raise $1 million.

In 1984, with the school's funds stretched thin, Wilson administrators decided to conduct the first real fundraising campaign since the "rebirth" of the school.

The meeting to decide about conducting a campaign was held in the office of the school's president, Mary-Linda Sorber Merriam. All attendees held mugs of hot water in their hands to stay warm. (The school was conserving heat to save money.)

The campaign was all about survival, sustainability, and building capacity. It was also about the leadership skills that Sarah Wilson envisioned when she initially funded the college.

The goal was to raise four times as much money than they ever raised before. The campaign was led by board member Ellie Allen (a passionate spokesperson for the school) and Nancy Besch (president of the Wilson College Alumnae Association). They also enlisted the help of Ben Conner (the then president of AMP Inc.).

Ellie, Nancy, and Mary-Linda played leading roles in the fund-raising campaign that not only reached but exceeded its goal, saving Wilson College and leading its recovery. They had the unwavering support of a loyal army of Wilson Women who just wouldn't quit.

The campaign's theme, "Standing as One," comes from the Wilson alma mater: "We will ever stand as one." The theme defined the Wilson Women who stood together to save the college they loved.

*You can read the story of Wilson College in the book* The College That Refused to Die, *by Mary-Linda Sorber Merriam Armacost, with help from Nancy Besch.*

This story speaks to the power volunteers can have when they come together in support of a worthy cause. I've also seen how a small group of individuals who dedicate themselves to doing it right can lead an organization to a level of success never achieved before.

## The Dream Team

In early 2004 I met Jim Leonard, head of school for Santa Fe Preparatory School ("Prep") in Santa Fe, New Mexico. Jim told me he wanted to conduct a comprehensive $10 million campaign. The school had conducted a $4 million campaign in the past, but it was a struggle.

Jim had a vision to expand the school's horizons. It needed a new library, more classroom space, campus renovations, and an endowment. It had a strong case for support and a respected leader in Jim.

The initial goal of the "Achieve the Dream" campaign was $7 million, the largest in Prep's history. The school had enough prospects to reach the goal if they were challenged, carefully cultivated, and made significant investments in the school's future.

Led by board chair Bill Conway and campaign cochairs Lee Ann Brown and Tim Lopez, a steering committee of board members, parents, and community leaders was enlisted to lead the campaign.

> **They respected each other, they were committed to each other, they held each other accountable, and they celebrated together.**

This "Dream Team" was perfect for the project. They each made a substantial gift. They worked together as a team, they respected each other, they were committed to each other, they held each other accountable, and they celebrated together. They did everything a volunteer committee should do.

As a result, the campaign was a huge success. The team secured the largest gifts Prep ever received and exceeded the goal by $1 million. This allowed them to build a library that earned Gold Leadership in Energy and Environmental Design (LEED) certification—the first building in New Mexico to do so. Governor Bill Richardson came to the campus to dedicate the building.

Since then, the school has completed another successful fundraising initiative and raised more than $3 million for a special endowment to honor Leonard's leadership.

Part of the success of the Dream Team can be attributed to staff who saw the value that volunteers bring to the campaign and who created a system to support their efforts every step of the way.

# Mutually Beneficial Volunteer Experiences

In most cases, you don't have to find volunteers—they find you.

That's because the best volunteers are mission-driven. They believe in what an organization does, and they want to help. It makes them feel good to be part of it. Motivations for giving and volunteering are often aligned, and people are often donors before they become volunteers.

Regardless of how they come to an organization, giving volunteers positive experiences requires thoughtful planning. This is especially important for fundraising in which the urgency to meet the campaign goal in a tight timeframe doesn't allow many missteps.

There are three critical steps for getting the most from volunteers in a campaign:

1. Clarify what is needed from volunteers. Enlisting volunteers without specifying what is expected from them can backfire. Most volunteers are busy, and if they don't feel their time is being respected and put to good use, their perception of the campaign—and potentially the organization—may be tarnished. Be cautious about asking for their advice; what is really needed is their help.

2. Recruit the right volunteers. Great donors don't always make good volunteers. Take the time to research every potential volunteer: check past and current volunteerism, review

names with board members to gather additional insights, and meet with them to gauge their potential.

3. Create an environment for success. A common misperception is that because volunteers donate their time and effort, they cost an organization nothing. That isn't true. Volunteers need to be activated through orientation, training, communication, and support. This requires time and resources.

## Champions for Your Cause

There are several roles volunteers can play in a campaign, but they should be united in a common cause—championing the organization and the campaign externally and internally.

If a volunteer is out in the community and someone says, "Hey, I hear the library is building a new wing," they need to be ready to respond by saying, "Yes, it's a great project, and we've been planning it for years. It's going to be wonderful for the community."

> **Volunteers can provide the entree that, when nurtured, can blossom into a lifelong relationship between the donor and the organization.**

The impact of volunteers in prospect development can't be overstated. They can facilitate access, engender trust, and influence giving levels. Some do it by meeting new people, and others do it through existing relationships. They can provide the entree that, when nurtured, can blossom into a lifelong relationship between the donor and the organization—the most valuable outcome for fundraising.

Sometimes volunteers need to be internal champions as well. It's important to have a few board members who are willing to stand up in a meeting and say, "This project can be valuable for the organization—it's important for us to do it." This brings needed credibility that isn't always achieved by a paid staff member. When a board member says it, their confidence in the organization and the campaign has real impact.

The Compass Group seeks out champions for all our clients. Their passion and dedication is persuasive and infectious.

# Expressing Appreciation

As important as any other aspect of working with volunteers is the everlasting rule: *Say thank you.* Many organizations struggle to show appreciation for their volunteers and donors. Here are a few insights that apply to both:

» **They want to be involved.** Share with them, communicate regularly, and include them in as many information sessions as possible.

» **They want to know their dollars have made a difference.** Show them how their donations helped the nonprofit reach important benchmarks, and share stories of those who have been impacted by the organization.

» **They want to know their dollars have been well spent.** Be transparent in reporting the specific ways the organization uses the funds they provided as well as funds they helped obtain from other donors.

Say thank you personally. A heartfelt, personal call or message from the CEO, the chair of the campaign, or a board member—

directly to the volunteer or donor—is really all they want. Visit with them personally whenever possible.

Supporting volunteers requires an investment of resources, and it's essential to invest in the overall fundraising operation as well. The fundraising team must be viewed as a business unit that generates income for the stability and sustainability of the entire nonprofit organization.

*"You must spend money
to make money."*

—TITUS MACCIUS PLAUTU

# CHAPTER 10

# IT TAKES MONEY TO RAISE MONEY

Many nonprofits I've known over the years are struggling financially. They're trying to become stable as they deliver on their mission, and they see increasing philanthropy as part of the solution. Philanthropy can and should be a significant revenue source for any worthy nonprofit, but *it takes money to raise money*. If an organization can make an investment in fundraising, it will pay big dividends.

For leaders of many nonprofits, it's difficult to divert funds from programs to an administrative function. If they have an earned revenue stream, they might carve out a budget for fundraising, but for organizations that rely on philanthropic support, limited fundraising income makes this type of investment impossible.

What's the solution? First, an organization must secure resources that can be invested in fundraising. Second, allocating more resources for fundraising must bring a significant return on that investment.

# Removing Restrictions

While most of my consulting work has focused on helping organizations fund specific goals through time-limited campaigns, one of the things I've valued most is unrestricted funding.

Unrestricted funds—those not designated for a specific program—can enable a nonprofit to take advantage of unique opportunities, address unexpected challenges, and invest in current and future stability. The value of access to unrestricted funds was highlighted over the past two years as the COVID-19 pandemic challenged the world. Here's an example:

I've been associated, in several capacities, with a worthy nonprofit for over forty years. I was there in the early '80s when it formed its first development office, and I've been involved as it progressed over the years. The organization always had a robust stream of earned income and never considered philanthropy a reliable funding source.

During the pandemic, this nonprofit had to suspend almost all earned income activities. As with many businesses, this put the organization at risk of not just closing but closing permanently. In response, the board and president quickly assessed the short- and long-term impact of the situation, then developed a strategy and budget that would ensure sustainability and a time-efficient way to resume operations when the time came.

This strategy relied on access to unrestricted philanthropic funds. Today, the organization is on the road to full recovery, and in the process, its leaders have come to understand the value of unrestricted philanthropy.

I've also worked with organizations that didn't appreciate the value of unrestricted support.

Not long ago, I was privileged to help a major arts organization with a $75 million campaign. They had a powerful, wealthy board of directors whose members were secure in their board positions and had grown accustomed to getting their way. Several board members had become the primary source of donations for specific programs. The development office supported those donors, and there were few major gift prospects in their portfolio who weren't current or past board members.

The organization had five different departments for programs, each with its own advisory board, and members of those boards were very loyal to their departments.

The campaign was structured to address priorities across the institution, and when it was announced, board members were the first to enthusiastically endorse it. They lined up to make significant contributions. To most fundraisers, this seems like a dream come true, but in fact, it was not.

Those gifts were unsolicited. They were volunteered by board members who largely ignored the priorities of the campaign and gave to programs that were their own priorities and pet projects. These powerful, influential board members sent a message: *We always have and will continue to do things our way.*

The administration was so glad to have these gifts that they didn't establish the boundaries needed to ensure the success of the overall campaign. They were unwilling or unable to say, "We're so grateful for your initial offer, but please hold off until we can visit with you personally. We want to meet with every board member to talk about how your philanthropic goals align with our priorities and our vision for the future."

Failure to address this issue at the beginning of the campaign had dire consequences. Board members continued to follow this pattern.

Many who had provided reliable, unrestricted support for years began to restrict their gifts instead. The pattern was repeated throughout the volunteer constituency.

When the campaign ended, the fundraising goal had been exceeded and the board celebrated—but it wasn't a success. Some objectives were overfunded, and others received little or no support. Many funded programs weren't priorities for the campaign, and little progress was made toward the vision for the future.

> *It's hard to imagine that a "successful" $75 million campaign would put an organization in jeopardy, but it did.*

But these were the least of the organization's problems. Because the campaign "hijacked" unrestricted giving, the institution suddenly faced a financial crisis—there were insufficient funds to support operations and ongoing programs, which put sustainability at risk.

It's hard to imagine that a "successful" $75 million campaign would put an organization in jeopardy, but it did. The organization survived the crisis and continues to operate, but it's a stark example of what can happen when unrestricted support isn't valued or prioritized by a nonprofit and its donors.

## The Angel Philanthropist

Fundraising for unrestricted gifts is hard, but imagine trying to convince a donor to contribute directly to the fundraising process—to give money so that more money can be raised. This is an incredibly difficult solicitation to make, and because of that, it rarely occurs.

That's not to say there aren't forward-thinking, self-motivated donors who will make this type of gift. There are, and attracting one of them is a game changer—in more ways than one.

While consulting with an independent school for their first campaign in a long time, it became clear that its development office had meager resources. Its low budget kept it from recruiting experienced development professionals and hindered it from implementing even the most basic fundraising strategies. If the school were to strengthen its annual giving program and conduct a $15 million campaign, it needed additional resources.

Its case for support was strongly endorsed by both internal and external constituents. Its prospects and donors believed in the vision for the school's future, so the decision was made to move forward with the campaign.

As we moved through planning and budgeting, it became clear that limited resources would be one of the biggest threats to getting the campaign off the ground.

The school had a donor who truly loved the institution and was grateful for the education her children received there. She was member of the board of trustees and had the capacity to be the lead donor in the campaign.

When she heard the school was struggling to fund the campaign, she not only volunteered to make the lead gift but earmarked part of that gift for increasing the capacity of the fundraising effort. She decided to become chair of the campaign, and in that role, she championed unrestricted giving and more investment in development.

Her understanding and commitment helped the development program evolve and grow and positioned it as a reliable source of funding for the school after the campaign ended.

It was her leadership—as donor, board member, and campaign chair—that influenced not only her fellow board members but 70 percent of all donors to make unrestricted gifts to the school.

Finding donors who understand the importance of sustainability and support it can dramatically change the trajectory of a nonprofit. Many organizations, however, have a difficult time justifying the "reinvestment" of philanthropy to improve fundraising.

# An Investment Opportunity

Without question, there is a direct correlation between investment and return for fundraising. It isn't the same for every nonprofit, but in many cases, as a fundraising program grows, so does the rate of return. Many might expect this to be enough justification for organizations to invest more in fundraising, but surprisingly it isn't.

Some organizations provide adequate resources, but many development offices operate on a shoestring budget, and some face budget cuts. I've been confronted with many explanations for this, and most of them reflect a lack of understanding about the power and value of philanthropy.

An executive director once said to me, "We can't put more resources into development because then we would have to invest the same amount in every department. We don't have the budget for that, and it wouldn't be fair." He was so worried about the optics that he didn't see the irony—an investment in fundraising would generate additional resources for all departments, ultimately reducing the disparity he was concerned about.

I've also heard "We have to make budget cuts next year, and we'll cut each department equally—by 10 percent." The leaders who make that kind of decision believe that strategy is equitable for everyone. If they thought it through, they would know that by cutting investment in a main revenue source, they risk reducing philanthropic income, making their problems worse, not better.

I've also worked with nonprofit boards that included finance professionals who were unable or unwilling to apply even the most basic investment principles to decision-making that would provide more for development.

As I worked with these organizations, I pursued different strategies to change their thinking, but I continued to run into the same roadblock: beyond the development team, no one considers return on investment or cost per dollar raised as part of budgeting or goal setting.

For most organizations, the expense of fundraising is a series of line items in the operating budget. Budget adjustments—both positive and negative—are usually calculated as a percentage and applied to fundraising expenses just like all other expenses.

Fundraising goals are usually set to reflect growth by percentage over the previous year—regardless of budget adjustments. Breaking these patterns is difficult but essential if an organization is going to grow philanthropy.

Why doesn't a positive return on investment or cost per dollar raised make it easier to invest in fundraising?

> *Money doesn't go out of and come back into the same bucket.*

Why doesn't a positive return on investment or cost per dollar raised make it easier to invest in fundraising? I believe it's because the money doesn't go out of and come back into the same bucket. Unless an organization makes unrestricted philanthropy the most important thing, fundraising doesn't necessarily provide resources that can be reinvested in raising more funds. Communicating this reality must be part of any case for maintaining or increasing a fundraising budget.

The most effective strategy I've found for connecting investment and return for fundraising is creating a detailed plan. This plan should include short- and long-term objectives, a financial goal, and a specific budget for every fundraising strategy. This allows those making budget decisions to see the direct impact that cuts will have on outcomes.

And even for new shops where fundraising is in its infancy, it will be hard to rationalize cutting $1 if it provides a return of even $1.10, especially when the long-term benefits are considered.

Employing this strategy isn't only helpful for budgeting; it can also ensure that resources invested in fundraising are aligned to philanthropic potential. Good stewardship demands this.

A monumental shift occurs the moment an organization moves from looking at fundraising as a budget expense to seeing it as an investment opportunity.

## Strategic Resource Investment

Determining *how much* and *how to* invest in development isn't easy. To do this well, it's important to understand the *philanthropic potential* of an organization. While this can be difficult, a time-limited campaign creates a unique opportunity to explore fundraising potential and align resources to maximize it.

As with other aspects of campaign planning and implementation, the gifts chart is a critical tool in making strategic investments in fundraising. Here are some examples:

1. An important data point from the gifts chart is the number of gifts needed for campaign success. When a three-to-one ratio is applied, the approximate number of prospects that must be solicited in a campaign will result. Armed with that information, address these questions:

(a) "Do we have the manpower—staff and volunteers—to effectively manage those prospects?" The answer to this question can guide resource investment decisions. (b) "How do we effectively share the case for supporting our campaign with all those prospects?" The answer to this question guides investments in communication materials, events, and travel for in-person meetings.

2. When a fundraising team goes through the exercise of "winning the campaign on paper"—which should be done often during the campaign—it will reveal gaps between the number of prospects identified and the number needed for success. Filling these gaps requires building the prospect pipeline by identifying and qualifying new prospects. Understanding the size of those gaps can guide decisions on resource investment, the use of demographic screening tools, and staff needed to utilize those tools well.

Resource investment decisions might be impacted by the campaign timeline. The budget for a multiyear campaign will differ from year to year to ensure the campaign is on track to achieve its goal in the established timeframe.

# Investing in Sustainability

Years ago, I was part of a consulting team that worked with a small liberal arts college. Our scope of work included building the school's fundraising capacity and conducting a campaign planning study. The school had an impressive history and dynamic leadership, but it was struggling financially.

Part of a larger network, the college had become the "poor stepchild," no longer contributing to the financial health of the network but relying on the other member institutions for support.

Although the college had conducted a successful fundraising campaign five years prior to our engagement, the alumni and development program was in its infancy. This was unusual; a successful campaign typically increases fundraising productivity even after it ends.

But this college had done something I never even imagined. After achieving the goal for the last campaign, it shuttered the development office. The entire staff was let go, all records were boxed up and sent to storage, and all outreach to alumni and donors ceased.

Because of this, the task ahead of us was extraordinary. The development staff was small, and they were new hires. Alumni and donor information was missing or incomplete, and records from the campaign couldn't be located.

This was an institution that, with a history of more than 150 years, was starting its alumni and development program from scratch and looking to philanthropy to fund immediate, significant financial needs. Though our efforts helped the cause by building a functional alumni and development program that secured large contributions, it turned out to be too little, too late.

The college was forced to close temporarily while leadership pursued a financial solution that didn't rely solely on philanthropy.

I think about that college often, and what stands out to me most is the lost opportunity, not only for philanthropy but also for nurturing an alumni constituency that would have supported the school in many ways.

Although that situation was extreme, it's a cautionary tale for organizations that put their philanthropic support at risk by under-resourcing the fundraising effort. Strategic resource investment is critical to success.

An organization can have all the resources in the world, but without strong, visionary leadership to orchestrate the fundraising effort, it won't come close to achieving its potential. Great leadership comes not only from top executives but from a wide—and sometimes surprising—variety of sources.

"*Leadership is being scared to death and saddling up anyway.*"

—JOHN WAYNE

# CHAPTER 11

# THE KEY INGREDIENT

Now that the keys to a successful fundraising campaign have been identified, I'll turn to the ingredient that pulls them all together—leadership.

To achieve success, a fundraising campaign, like any other business initiative, must have strong, capable leadership. Great leaders don't just provide organization and direction for the many tasks in a campaign; they inspire and motivate the fundraising team as well.

Donors gravitate to respected, visionary leadership. They want to be guided, they want to be inspired, and they want to believe their gifts will be used wisely to have an impact on their community, maybe even the world.

Donors look for leadership at nonprofit organizations in four places:

» **The CEO.** This leader must have a vision and a plan and be able to articulate them in an inspiring way. The CEO needs to build an enthusiastic, skilled, and diverse staff and be willing to include other leadership outside of their own.

» **The governing board.** The board must consist of respected, responsible individuals who can be trusted. They must consistently communicate that they believe in and support the CEO and set a positive example through words and deeds that others can follow.

» **The development staff.** This team must interact with prospective donors in a positive, knowledgeable way that inspires confidence and leads to investments in the organization. The staff must have the experience needed to respond to unexpected changes with creative strategies and tactics.

» **The champions.** Donors look for people in a nonprofit's constituency who are "champions." These people step out and are vocal about their support for the campaign and the fundraising team, and they invite others to join them in the effort.

I've been fortunate to witness superior leadership throughout my career.

## Superior Leadership

Hanging on the wall of my office is a framed report that includes the final totals for "Commitment to Excellence," a campaign conducted by the University of Mississippi from January 1994 to December 2000. As a consultant to that campaign, I had the opportunity to work with one of the most effective leaders I have ever met—Robert Khayat.

I consider Khayat to be somewhat of a Renaissance man. He has two degrees—a bachelor's and a law degree, both from Mississippi. He is an author and musician, and he played professional football in the NFL.

After a time as a professor in the law school, Khayat was appointed the fifteenth chancellor of the University of Mississippi in 1995. He assumed this role with a bold vision for the future. He believed the institution could be a "Great American Public University." At the time, it was not regarded as such.

One of Khayat's first initiatives was establishing a Phi Beta Kappa chapter at the university. The school's past applications for a chapter were rejected for many reasons, the biggest of which were racial issues and the association of the school with the rebel flag.

While Khayat appreciated the benefits that an Honors College would bring to the university—attracting the best and the brightest, not just from Mississippi but from across the nation—he saw beyond that.

He saw an opportunity to build unity around a critical issue that needed to be addressed if his vision had any chance of becoming a reality. The university needed to acknowledge and reconcile a difficult history.

---

*"I really did have a vision, and I could see—I could see what we could be if we could commit to doing it. And that we could gain national respect and internal respect for ourselves and for the state. We could be a bright light."*

—Robert Khayat

---

During his tenure, the university removed all Confederate symbols from campus; erected a monument dedicated to James Meredith, the first Black man to enroll in the university; and secured a Phi Beta Kappa charter.

Khayat not only had a vision for the university and a commitment to making it a reality but also recognized the power of philanthropy and wasn't afraid to ask for financial help. Early on, he found champions for his cause in Jim and Sally Barksdale. Jim was founder of the computer services company Netscape, and the couple's multimillion-dollar gift was instrumental in establishing the Honors College.

As evidenced by the report on my wall, however, this was only the beginning. Khayat initiated the Commitment to Excellence campaign shortly after becoming chancellor. With a goal of $200 million, donations were designated for a variety of projects, including a new law school.

To ensure success, Khayat invested in fundraising. There were only a few people on the school's development staff, and it became part of my work to help them build a top-notch operation by hiring and training twenty-five fundraisers and recruiting and training a large, varied group of volunteers.

Throughout his tenure, Khayat built relationships with many loyal graduates, including very wealthy ones. He had no difficulty asking a high-level corporate executive or a successful entrepreneur for $10 million for the law school that meant so much to him.

During the campaign, university alumni practically lined up to make donations, equally motivated by their love of the school and their desire to see Khayat succeed. In the final accounting, the campaign raised more than $540 million against that $200 million goal, and progress toward Khayat's vision of becoming a Great American Public University was well underway.

During Khayat's fourteen-year tenure, the university raised almost $1 billion. He succeeded because he had qualities that any great leader must possess. He had a vision for a university that is beloved by its alumni; the courage to challenge the school to be great;

the respect and admiration of many people who helped him eradicate symbols of racism from campus; a willingness to ask for financial help; and the humility to make sure people knew this was not for him but for the university and the state of Mississippi.

---

*"I wanted to get this job done for the joy of doing it. If someone asks how I would like to be remembered, I guess I would want them to say I was kind, that I tried to be respectful and kind."*

—Robert Khayat

---

I'm grateful for the opportunity to work with this great leader who accomplished so much.

## Surprising Sources of Leadership

There are cases in which essential leadership doesn't come from an executive or a board of directors; it comes from donors.

I consulted with a community hospital in upstate New York that wanted to do a $15 million fundraising campaign. After we conducted a planning study for the project, the hospital's leadership—the board of directors and the fundraising team—stated that the goal was impossible. They said they didn't have the capacity to achieve it and recommended that the campaign be postponed.

But a small group of donors saw things differently. They came forward and expressed their affection for the hospital; they said they'd do anything to raise money and reach the goal. Three of the donors said they would each provide lead gifts, totaling more than $10 million.

The donors wanted to support the hospital because of the quality of care it provided and the nursing staff and physicians, who were integral parts of the community. Many people cared about the place.

> *Fundraisers must be alert, recognize leadership when they see it, and support those who are willing and able to step up.*

Because of the outspoken leadership from donors, hospital executives changed course. They went ahead with the fundraising campaign and exceeded the original goal.

Leadership can come from a variety of places. Fundraisers must be alert, recognize leadership when they see it, and support those who are willing and able to step up.

## Fundraising Leadership

While there is no shortage of guidance out there on what makes a great leader, I've often found it helpful to translate that specifically to fundraising.

When I talk with boards about what it takes to conduct a successful campaign, they always want to know what it means for them. They want to know what they will be expected to do, and most have anxiety about fulfilling those expectations.

That anxiety, if not addressed up front and honestly, may manifest itself in some board members dragging their feet and pushing back with questions and statements like "Why do we have to do this now?" or "Aren't there other things that have to get done before we start a campaign?" or "I don't think I'm the right board member for this organization."

But when expectations are made clear, most board members don't find them onerous at all. The best leaders find a way to meet and even exceed them. The expectations include the following:

» **Endorse the campaign.** Entering into a campaign is a leadership decision to work toward a vision by funding the initiative. Great leaders not only endorse a well-conceived campaign but also readily share their enthusiasm for the organization and campaign every chance they get.

» **Advocate.** Leaders are the primary advocates for a campaign. They're asked to step up in a variety of ways to promote the vision and campaign priorities. The best leaders learn the case for support and present it to others in the context of their own personal story.

» **Make a gift.** Leaders set the example with their own philanthropic support. A campaign can create a pivotal moment for leaders as they consider their engagement with the organization in the context of making a significant campaign gift. Leaders may struggle as they consider significant philanthropic expectations, and some may question whether they should remain in a leadership role. Board members and campaign leaders need to know three things when it comes to their own giving:

1. Giving is proportional: philanthropic gifts from leaders should align with both their commitment to the organization and their financial ability. The goal is to have everyone make the same gift—not in size, but as a shared reflection of commitment and ability. Each board member should be asked to make a gift by another board member

who has already made a gift. Some leaders will be top ten donors, while others will not; but all great leaders make a commitment of which they can be proud.

2. Board giving is first, not more: we ask board members to make their own gifts to the campaign first—before others who are outside the organization are asked. The methodology for determining the ask amount for a board member is the same as it is for any other prospect. Board members are simply asked to do it first. Board giving will set the philanthropic example and establish the pace for the campaign.

3. Annual support and campaign support are different: annual gifts support operations. An annual gift to an organization typically comes from discretionary income. Again, it is proportionate: those with significant ability are asked to participate at a higher level than those with lesser ability. These gifts are made every year and are typically "written in full from a checkbook." Campaign gifts support aspirations. Campaign gifts are an investment in the future of the organization. These gifts are typically sourced from a donor's assets and planned over several years. If a campaign commitment can be paid from a checkbook, the donor was likely not asked for a big enough commitment. During a campaign, donors will be asked to provide both annual and campaign support.

» **Identify others.** Campaign success depends on having enough prospects. Leaders are expected to help identify prospects within their personal and professional spheres of influence. They may also be asked to review lists of existing prospects and give confidential insights that help establish and build relationships. Great leaders seek opportunities to connect individuals with worthy organizations.

» **Cultivate.** Leaders are often in the best position to cultivate prospects. They can speak confidently and passionately about the organization and the campaign, and they often have more access to a prospect than fundraising staff. Leaders will be asked to deepen relationships between prospects and organizations and take planned and unplanned opportunities to do that.

» **Solicit.** Leaders will be asked to serve on fundraising teams and ask for campaign commitments. "Peer-to-peer" solicitation is the most successful, not only for securing gifts but for maximizing the gift amounts as well. Great leaders develop their own comfort level and style in asking for a gift; always ask for the desired amount; and follow up in an appropriate, timely fashion.

» **Steward.** Leaders will be asked to express appreciation to donors for their commitments. Great leaders recognize the importance of this step, and they stand ready to be the messenger whenever they're needed.

It would be wonderful if every leader stepped up and played all these roles in a campaign, but that's very unlikely. The best will figure out what is needed most and how they can have the biggest impact, and they will deliver on those things as they lead the campaign to success.

They will also determine a critical factor for themselves and their organization—the level of risk they will take on. Effectively balancing the risk-reward equation is an essential—and sometimes unsettling—part of campaigning.

*"Fortune favors the brave."*

—VIRGIL

## CHAPTER 12

# LAYING IT ON
# THE LINE

I'm a true believer that taking calculated risks can be life changing. This guided my early work in experiential education, and I've seen the impact, not only on those who take risks but on those who bear witness.

## *Personal Risk and Reward*

This reminds me of Judy, a forty-year-old mother of four who worked as an administrative assistant in a school district in Connecticut. That district partnered with my nonprofit, the Adventure Challenge School, to provide experiential learning programs for their students.

The programs used real-life experiences to show kids the connection between academics and experience—where real learning begins. There were challenging activities such as sailing, caving, climbing, winter camping, and urban adventures.

Judy was recently divorced and looking for a challenge, an experience that would test her limits. She knew us well, so when we took our "junior leaders"—kids who helped us with the Adventure Challenge

School throughout the year—on a backpacking trip in the Wind River Range of the Wyoming Rockies, she asked to join us.

Even though she was a novice hiker, we thought her grit and determination would make her a good fit for the team, and since everyone else in the group was younger and in better shape than her, we knew we could help her with the physical part of the trip.

A bunch of us—fourteen junior leaders, three adult trip leaders, and Judy—drove across the country in a big, green school bus and started our backpacking trek in Lander, Wyoming. The hike went well. We enjoyed having Judy with us, and she was both a willing participant and "Mom" to anyone who needed her. She became a valued part of the team.

The trip was a lot of fun, but it was very challenging. Everyone had to pitch in and help each other with route finding, food rationing, maintaining a good pace, setting up and taking down camp, and leaving no trace as our enthusiastic team made its way through the mountains.

The highlight of the trip was a climb to the top of Wind River Peak. At just about thirteen thousand feet high, the peak isn't a technically difficult climb, but there was a significant rise in elevation from our campsite to the summit. We thought it would be a great feeling to start in the dark and reach the summit in time for sunrise. That was our plan.

The day before our climb to the summit, we went rock climbing in a valley near our camp. The climbs there were fifty to seventy-five feet and could be "belayed," with a safety rope looping from the top of the climb down to the climber who wears a secure harness at the bottom. As the climber ascends, the "belayer" at the top takes up slack in the rope, shortening the distance a climber would fall if they lost their footing.

There are protocols on both ends of the rope to ensure safety, but the climbs, which can be almost vertical, are intimidating for someone standing at the base of the cliff and looking up.

On that day, it was misty and overcast, and the climbs turned out to be more difficult than we anticipated. Even the strongest kids struggled and took much longer than expected. They knew, however, that they had accomplished something very difficult when they reached the top.

I was concerned about whether Judy could do the climb. I put her at the end of the line of climbers. That way, if the weather got bad, she would have a way out. But the weather held, and when Judy got her chance, she wanted to give it a try.

Judy fastened into the climbing harness at the bottom, put on her helmet, communicated with her belayer, and began. She struggled from the very beginning. She was safe and in good hands, but she had never done anything like this before and looked afraid.

When she got halfway up the climb, she stopped. Clearly, she was very tired. She looked up at me, rested for a minute, then grabbed the next handhold and foothold on the rock face. She took another short rest, but she struggled with her next steps—reaching her limit. I considered giving her the choice to downclimb or be lowered in her harness from above, but as it turned out, I didn't have to.

Suddenly, something wonderful happened. The semicircle of cliffs allowed other climbers to look down and see Judy on the rock face. The kids who made it to the top saw her struggling. All at once, they started yelling, encouraging her to keep going, to keep trying, telling her that she could do it.

This was no rah-rah pep talk. They were literally screaming at the top of their lungs, using all their energy, passion, profanity, and love for Judy to propel her up the rock face.

Little by little, handhold by handhold, Judy took in their energy and pushed herself. As I watched, I saw her expression change from exhausted and fearful to focused and determined. Somehow, she kept going.

When she literally dragged herself over the top of the cliff and slowly stood up and released herself from the safety system, she was engulfed by the rest of the team. Everyone was shouting, laughing, crying, and celebrating the fact that Judy made it to the top.

> *Taking great risks—both physical and psychological—can yield great rewards.*

Then, at that moment, the dark clouds broke, and a spectacular rainbow appeared right in front of us. It was like a miracle.

All our lives were changed that day, and it happened because Judy overcame her fear and took the risk. Physically, she started out as the "weakest link" of the group, but her belief in herself and her grit inspired our confidence, respect, and admiration for her.

I'm sure none of us will ever forget Judy's climb that day. It was a real-life example of how taking great risks—both physical and psychological—can yield great rewards.

## Campaign Risk and Reward

While Judy's story is one of personal triumph, I believe there is inherent risk for every organization that decides to conduct a fundraising campaign. For those that do, the rewards go far beyond the money raised.

As a consultant, I've spent a great deal of time helping my clients identify, assess, and mitigate the risk of having a failed campaign. The

Compass Group business model is designed to ensure the highest probability of success for our clients, and our consultants are trained to quickly identify and address potential risks to campaign progress.

But if the COVID-19 pandemic has taught us anything over the last two years, it's that there are risks we can't predict, and they can be difficult to manage.

The risk tolerance of nonprofit organizations varies greatly. For some, both known and unknown risks are paralyzing, and they can't move forward. But those that reap the biggest rewards face considerable risk and forge ahead anyway, like the Wyoming chapter of The Nature Conservancy.

## Wild and Working

In 2008, the Wyoming chapter was considering the most significant fundraising campaign in its history. The planning study we conducted recommended a five-year campaign with a goal of $40 million. For a variety of reasons, however, this wasn't an easy move for them to make.

> » The economy was in a terrible place. Many established financial institutions were in trouble. In fact, on the day that chapter leadership voted to go forward with a campaign, the global financial services firm Lehman Brothers disappeared.

> » State Director Andrea Erickson-Quiroz and Director of Philanthropy Molly Hampton were new to their roles.

> » Previous leadership mainly engaged in transactional giving as opposed to building long-term relationships. Donors were neglected, relationships waned, and stewardship of gifts was average at best.

» The board and staff had little to no campaign experience and limited expertise in face-to-face solicitation.

The chapter had never considered a campaign of this size, and, understandably, the staff was afraid of failing.

But the group was blessed with visionary leaders like board chair Paige Williams and volunteers Anne Pendergast and Anne Young. They were passionate and determined. After carefully weighing the risks and considering the critical conservation needs of Wyoming, the board voted to move forward with the campaign.

> **The entire organization adopted the motto "Put the donor first."**

That showed courage, a belief in each other, and the determination to provide what the state desperately needed.

To give the campaign the highest chance of success, we worked together to devise a creative plan of action that gave them time to learn, strategize, build a team, and develop relationships that would be essential. The entire organization adopted the motto "Put the donor first."

Moving forward with the campaign turned out to be one of the best decisions the chapter ever made. Beyond having an over-the-goal campaign success, the chapter benefited in many ways:

» They triumphed over the fear of failure.

» They built a high-functioning development program that supported the campaign, strengthened the annual fund, and positioned the chapter for future fundraising success.

» They created successful fundraising teams consisting of board members, staff, and volunteers. Those teams supported each other like no other organization I've seen. They built a trust and openness that is rare. They helped each other succeed.

» They developed a track record of success in major gift fundraising. One of their most reticent volunteer fundraisers turned into the most outspoken supporter of the chapter, its work, and the importance of asking for a gift.

» They effectively engaged board members in the campaign. The board's efforts to make progress and willingness to help were very impressive.

» They established a culture of philanthropy and were invested in building lifelong relationships with their donors.

» They demonstrated that they cared about their donors and let them know they were part of a larger family of conservationists in Wyoming.

» They made fundraising personal, which led to a $1 million commitment in the last week of the campaign from a donor who wasn't even a prospect when the campaign began.

As a result of that success, more board members were willing to take leadership roles in fundraising, which led to another campaign—a larger one—that began after a year of planning. With Margie Taylor as the board chair, four different board members led the second campaign—Linda Murchison, Frank Goodyear, Mary Anne Dingus, and David Work. Their efforts resulted in over-the-goal success for the $50 million campaign.

We balance risk and reward in every campaign we take on. The Wyoming chapter had the vision and courage to understand where they were and where they wanted to be. They found that the risks actually served as opportunities to grow and become more sustainable. They committed themselves to the work that needed to be done, worked hard, relied on each other, and held each other accountable. In the end, the rewards far outweighed the risks.

Like all fundraising teams, the Wyoming chapter followed its planning, preparation, and execution with an inevitable task that many people find difficult: asking for money. In all fundraising campaigns, everything boils down to making the ask. It has to be done, and it has to be done the right way.

*"Fundraising doesn't begin until someone asks someone else for money."*

—SY SEYMOUR, DESIGNS FOR FUND-RAISING

## CHAPTER 13

# THE PERFECT ASK

People always want to know "How do I ask someone for a gift?" Most folks have anxiety about asking and would like to find a comfortable way to do it. They hope there are "magic words" or a step-by-step formula. But, trust me, there aren't.

There are many ways to make an effective ask, and I always recommend preparation and practice, but before worrying about getting it perfect, the focus needs to be on getting it done at all. It's not always easy.

## *"I Can't Beg for Money"*

Brother Theodore Drahmann, who was president of Christian Brothers University in Memphis, Tennessee, was a respected, lifelong educator, an effective business manager, and an honest, pious man.

He did many great things in his life, but there was one thing he absolutely would not do under any circumstances: ask someone for money.

Years ago, I had the opportunity to work with "Brother Ted." My friend Nick Scully was vice president for advancement at Christian

Brothers University, and I consulted on their $15 million campaign for a new business school.

The main prospect for the lead gift of $3 million was a woman named Mertie Buckman. Mertie's husband Bob founded Buckman Labs in Memphis. The success of the company allowed the Buckmans to make large donations to organizations they cared about.

Mertie, who was on the board of directors of the university, had a great deal of respect for Brother Ted, and they got along well. Mertie knew about the plans for the business school and how important it was.

As the leader of the school, it was up to Brother Ted to approach Mertie about making the lead gift. At that time, it would have been the largest gift in the university's history.

When Nick and I asked him to do this, he said, "I'm sorry, but I just can't do it. It's demeaning for me to ask someone for a gift—I feel like I'm begging. If she wants to make a gift, she'll just do it. Why do I have to ask her?"

## Finding a Comfort Zone

For months, Nick and I struggled to get Brother Ted to change his mind. Nick tried everything to make him more comfortable. They role-played the conversation at least a dozen times. But whenever Brother Ted got to the point of asking for $3 million, he would stop and say, "I can't say it. I just can't. I would be begging for money. This is just not for me."

Nick suggested that, instead of verbally asking for $3 million, Brother Ted could show Mertie the gifts chart with the $15 million campaign goal and simply point to the top of the chart. But Brother Ted didn't buy it: "I don't know, Nick. Even just pointing to a gift of that amount doesn't feel right."

As difficult as this was for Brother Ted, we had to remind him that, as head of the university, it was his responsibility to meet with the most generous donors and solicit the largest gifts. To prevent the campaign from being derailed, Nick and I decided we couldn't delay any longer. A meeting was arranged for Brother Ted, Mertie, and Nick. Nick was ready to step in if Brother Ted couldn't make the ask.

## The Moment of Truth

The luncheon meeting occurred during the Christmas season, and when the group got together, their interaction was friendly and effortless. Brother Ted easily steered the conversation to the plans for the new business school and the value it would bring to the university.

And then, the moment was upon them. After all the effort to make Brother Ted comfortable—the role play, the practice, the props—it was time for him to ask for the gift.

Nick watched as Brother Ted held up the gifts chart. He hesitated, then he pointed to the lead gift of $3 million at the top of the chart. He seemed unable to speak, and Nick considered jumping in and making the ask himself. But suddenly Brother Ted said, "Mertie, it's my hope that you will consider being the angel on top of our Christmas tree."

Smiling, Mertie replied, "You know, Brother Theodore, I think I can do that."

> **Anyone can do it, but preparation and practice are musts.**

This was a prime example of the "perfect ask." In spite of his discomfort, Brother Ted found a way to make it happen. He made it personal, spoke from his heart, and treated Mertie with respect and affection. Making the request in this way not only suited him, but it also suited the season and, most importantly, the donor—and Mertie said, "Yes."

There are many ways to ask for a gift, and I believe anyone can do it, but preparation and practice are musts.

# Tips for Making the Perfect Ask

Anyone on the front lines asking for significant gifts owes it to the prospective donor and the nonprofit organization to do it well. This requires both preparation and practice. Each prospect deserves a well-planned, personalized approach that brings together inspiration and impact. Here's some guidance on positioning volunteers for the greatest success:

> » **Make sure volunteers know and can communicate the case for support.** It's important that they convey the importance of the campaign in their own words. They need to speak from the heart. If they can make their appeal personal, they will be powerful advocates.

> » **Secure the volunteer's commitment before they solicit others.** Being able to speak of their commitment, especially when it's aligned with their ability to give, is incredibly persuasive when seeking equally generous gifts from others.

> » **Be intentional about engaging volunteers.** There are many factors to consider when determining whether a volunteer should solicit a prospective donor. The bottom line is it's best to use the person or people who will inspire the greatest generosity.

» **Include volunteers in developing solicitation plans.** Volunteers involved in developing a plan to solicit a prospect will understand the strategy better and be more likely to fulfill the critical role they play in it. They often develop a sense of ownership for the plan and its success.

» **Fully brief volunteers on the prospect and the plan.** Knowing who the prospect is; how they were identified, qualified, and cultivated; and how the ask amount was determined will build a volunteer's confidence in the solicitation process.

» **Have volunteers solicit their best prospect first.** A successful first ask will raise confidence and motivate a volunteer to participate in future solicitations.

» **Have volunteers reach out to schedule meetings.** The volunteer may have more success in securing a meeting with a promising prospect than a staff person would. When this is the case, the volunteer should contact the prospect personally to set the date and time, be honest about the purpose of the meeting, and be clear about who will attend.

» **Schedule face-to-face, in-person solicitations.** Solicitations are most successful when done face-to-face and in-person. Work closely with the volunteer to schedule an in-person solicitation in an ideal setting.

» **Train volunteers to be effective solicitors.** Solicitation calls tend to make volunteers' hands sweat, so it's important to give them guidance and opportunities to put that guidance into practice. I recommend regular role-playing to increase their comfort level with all aspects of solicitation:

» **Setting the tone.** Relax and set a conversational and friendly tone from the start.

» **Leading the conversation.** Master the art of small talk and avoid long silences.

» **Sharing your story.** Be genuine and show passion for the organization.

» **Promoting the case.** Learn to weave campaign talking points into the conversation.

» **Being direct and specific.** Be straightforward and make the specific ask in a way that is respectful of the donor. Here are some suggestions:

  » "Would you consider making a leadership gift of $_____ to be paid over three to five years?"

  » "Will you join me/us by making a gift of $_____?"

» **Negotiating.** Maintain control of the ask, and give options as a way of negotiating the highest gift amount. Negotiation tactics include

  » providing multiyear payment options;

  » outlining the level and number of gifts necessary for the campaign to be successful;

  » emphasizing the importance of setting a leadership example;

  » sharing details about the number and size of other commitments that have been made (and by whom, if appropriate);

  » describing the impact their gift will have for the organization and the campaign;

» introducing potential opportunities for the donor to be recognized for their gift; and

» suggesting alternative ways to give.

» **Handling objections.** A "no" isn't always a "No!" Sometimes "no" means "I need you to convince me" or "Not now." In those situations, it's important to keep the lines of communication open by responding to objections with sensitivity and clarity. Suggested responses are illustrated in the following table.

| OBJECTION | SUGGESTED RESPONSE |
|---|---|
| "We already give to so many organizations. How can we give significantly to this effort?" | "I know you do. My family and I had to consider our commitment in light of many similar requests. We decided that this project is a top priority for us right now. We hope you will agree." |
| "You're asking me to give much more than I've ever considered giving to [organization]." | "You're not alone—I was surprised by the amount I was asked to consider. But I found that by spreading my pledge over three years or more, my semiannual payments are not as big a burden as I assumed they would be." |

| OBJECTION | SUGGESTED RESPONSE |
|---|---|
| "Who said I could give this much?" | "The 'ask amount' was recommended by an anonymous group of our peers after lengthy deliberation. We're not telling you what to give; we're hoping you'll consider a commitment at this level as you consider a multiyear pledge that aligns with your interest in [organization] and your ability to give." |
| "I can't make a decision now. I'll have to talk it over with _____." | "Of course. I hope you do. May I see you at the same time next week to continue our discussion? We're working under a deadline—I hope you'll help me meet it." |
| "I can't afford to give now—maybe later." | "I'm glad you want to support [organization]. Why not pledge now and start your payments later in the year or next year? We've also accepted gifts and pledges of appreciated assets, such as securities and real estate, if that is better for you." |
| "The recent economic activity has left me wary about making a commitment." | "All pledges are made in good faith, in the belief that you will be able to fulfill them. All of us supporting this project have the option to cancel or increase our pledges at any time should our circumstances change." |

» **Practicing patience.** Some gifts may require more than one meeting. Patience may be helpful in closing the solicitation at or close to the desired level.

» **Documenting the commitment.** It's important to confirm the commitment in writing.

» **Reporting on progress.** The details and outcome of a solicitation should be captured and reported back to the organization as quickly as possible.

» **Sharing success.** Success builds campaign momentum. Share and celebrate successful outcomes.

» **Showing appreciation.** It's important to express appreciation to the donor for their commitment.

» **Making friends.** Regardless of the outcome of the solicitation, the interaction is an important step in building a potentially lifelong relationship with the prospect.

Implementing these steps will help prepare anyone to be an effective solicitor, but in the end, it's critical to remember that the essence of "the perfect ask" is simplicity:

» Tell your prospect why the organization is important to you.

» Tell your prospect why you volunteered to help the organization meet its goal and why you invest in it.

» Tell your story, and speak from the heart.

» Then just ask them to join you.

The perfect ask is the volunteer's ask, from their heart, with sincerity and passion. When they make it personal, they can't make a mistake.

Volunteers who are willing to ask others to support a fundraising campaign are a huge asset. Those who are able to achieve a level of comfort, find their own voice, and get it done will be the key to campaign success. Invest in them, support them, nurture them, and celebrate them!

> *The perfect ask is the volunteer's ask, from their heart, with sincerity and passion.*

Even dedicated volunteers must be held accountable. They need someone to remind them of deadlines for the many short-term goals embedded in a campaign. They need to be under the watchful eye of someone playing the role of the overseer, the "insistent voice."

"Each person holds so much power within themselves that needs to be let out. Sometimes they need a little nudge, a little direction and just a little coaching—and the greatest things can happen."

—PETE CARROLL, NFL FOOTBALL COACH

CHAPTER 14

# THE INSISTENT VOICE

When I began my fundraising consulting career at Ketchum in the early 1980s, I was introduced to campaign direction by the people who started the profession. Through their example and my own work, I realized one of the most important things a fundraising consultant can do is ensure that things that need to get done actually get done. I discovered the best way to do this was to be "the insistent voice."

Successful execution of a campaign requires leaders, volunteers, and staff to come together to accomplish multiple tasks concurrently according to a deadline-driven plan. This work must be pursued over and above the day-to-day business of development, which continues during the campaign.

Organizations often struggle to coordinate and balance this work, and while a consultant can help by clarifying and assigning tasks, often the most valuable role we play is ensuring tasks are completed in a timely, effective manner.

As the outside expert, fundraising counsel can hold anyone and everyone in a campaign accountable. We bring the external stimulus and objectivity needed to push leadership and volunteers to conduct solicitations, close gifts, and ultimately reach the campaign goal on time. We can be the insistent voice that asks these hard questions:

- » "Have you done what you said you will do?"

- » "When will it happen?"

- » "Have you asked for the right amount?"

- » "When will you get your prospect to agree to make their gift?"

- » "What more do you need?"

- » "How can we help?"

- » "Have you done your best?"

To ensure progress, I've often had conversations with nonprofit leaders—executive directors, presidents, and board chairs—about their own performance in a campaign. Sometimes they just need some reassurance, sometimes they need instruction, sometimes they need to vent to an objective listener, and sometimes they need to be prompted to provide leadership. Part of our job as fundraising counsel is to provide the insistent voice that turns good intentions into action.

## Stepping In

Early in my career, I had an experience with a major public university that conducted the largest campaign any such university had done over a three-year period. My role was campaign director, and I was on-site full-time for three years. As the campaign started, a steering committee was formed by the campaign chair and the president of the university.

The committee consisted of two former governors, a former vice president of the United States, twelve CEOs of multinational corporations, and several philanthropic leaders. It was an intimidating group of people, and our first task was to identify prospects for the top gifts in the campaign.

This group had never been in the same room together, and as they engaged in small talk and enjoyed the camaraderie, they also ate up valuable time. We had only ninety minutes for what we called "prospect review."

Someone had to get them to focus and get the work done, and that someone was me.

It took me a while to figure out what to say, but finally I cleared my throat and said loudly, "Gentlemen, I'm so pleased to see you all here today and glad to see you catching up with each other. Our president, campaign chair, and others have obligations later this afternoon, and we have just ninety minutes to get our work done. If we could get down to business, we can get you out of here on time."

It worked like magic. They all quieted down and went to work. I led them through the process, got them out of there early, and earned their confidence. In that first interaction, as the insistent voice, I demonstrated my ability to focus on a task, complete it in a timely manner, and respect their time and effort in the process. Being the insistent voice earned me credibility and respect. That served me well throughout the campaign, especially when I needed their help with other things.

> Being the insistent voice earned me credibility and respect.

Regardless of their high-level status, they wanted leadership and direction, and they felt good about accomplishing our task.

# Passing the Torch

The need for an external expert to ensure accountability can be essential at the start of a campaign, but the ultimate goal is to have the organization learn to hold itself accountable. This will benefit the current campaign, and, as their fundraising capacity grows, it will benefit campaigns in the future.

The story of St. Anne's School in Maryland is a good illustration of how the insistent voice can lead to campaign success and be a catalyst for lasting organizational change.

The leaders at St. Anne's started their campaign planning the right way. They hired a consulting firm to conduct a planning study, they completed a strategic plan to identify funding priorities, and the board committed to supporting the campaign.

But things got off track. When the consulting firm reported the results of the study to the board, the firm recommended a fundraising strategy that wasn't right for the school. The strategy didn't address some of the unique challenges facing St. Anne's.

The school had its share of problems: the relationship between the board and staff was strained, there were major concerns about the priorities in the strategic plan, and philanthropic support had declined in recent years.

Unfortunately, these issues were practically ignored by the consultants. The recommendations they proposed were generic and presented without conviction or enthusiasm. As a result, the board and steering committee were hesitant to ask prospects for donations.

They worried about conflicting messages and were afraid they wouldn't get it right, embarrassing themselves, the school, and their donors. Campaign progress was almost at a standstill when Compass became involved.

As we learned of the school's bad experience with fundraising counsel, we knew we needed to tread lightly in our role as the insistent voice. In the first few months, a lot of time was spent listening and learning. This served us well as we formed a partnership founded on communication, leadership, structure, and creativity.

As we prepared to launch the campaign, we developed a plan that included specific tasks and deadlines. We combined that with detailed roles and responsibilities for everyone involved in the effort. This information was widely circulated. We made sure everyone understood the campaign plan and knew what they were expected to do. Understanding how it all worked helped to promote a sense of ownership that didn't exist before.

To establish discipline and accountability, we introduced regular "check-ins," and monthly meetings were planned for each board member, staff member, and volunteer. We were clear about what to expect in each meeting, and we provided guidance on how to prepare.

The meetings were very effective. People understood their roles, we supported them in their efforts, and they were held accountable according to an agreed-upon timetable. Our insistent voice prompted—with few exceptions—board members, staff members, and volunteers to fulfill their expectations. And the campaign started to make significant progress.

This helped the group build confidence and trust, not just in us but in each other. As they made progress, they became invested in making more, and they began holding themselves and each other accountable for maintaining the momentum. It was an incredible thing to see, and it spoke to the shared commitment for making their vision a reality.

St. Anne's School achieved the campaign goal in the defined timeframe. Enthused about the fundraising experience, the school's board, administrators, staff, and donors expressed that they were ready to do it again, and they wanted to do it bigger and better next time.

# One Step at a Time

Serving as the insistent voice requires respect for the organization's team as well as diplomacy and balance. It's important to respect that people are doing the best they can and won't always be successful. Be diplomatic when pushing leaders and volunteers for results. Strive for a reasonable balance between good outcomes and bad ones.

Campaigns can be complex, but they can be implemented one step at a time. It's rare that every step is completed on schedule, but it's not helpful to relentlessly push the team forward. Stepping back at times to celebrate what has been accomplished—as opposed to harping on what hasn't been done—is often the very thing that will motivate people to forge ahead.

> **Respect that people are doing the best they can and won't always be successful.**

Years ago, my wife and I did a climb of Mount Kenya in Africa. Hoping to reach the summit by sunrise, we began to climb in the dark. Other than the frozen incline in front of us, we couldn't see a thing on the way to the top, but we followed in the footsteps of our experienced guide.

Every now and then, sensing we were behind and anxious to gauge our progress, we would look up at him and say, "Where are we?"

And every time, he looked back at us and said reassuringly, "You are where you're supposed to be."

This is our message to people who take on the challenge of a fundraising campaign with hopes of achieving a great vision for the organizations they serve. While we help to chart the path forward, remind them of where they are along the way, reinforce positive behaviors, celebrate successes, and address challenges promptly as they appear, we—and they—can only do so much.

At some point, they need to take the lead. They will be the messenger, reminding everyone in their group, "We are where we're supposed to be."

*"The business of development says, 'It doesn't matter how much money you raised this year—you have to raise more money next year.'"*

—ANONYMOUS

CHAPTER 15

# THE MORNING AFTER

Yesterday was the last day of the campaign. The goal was achieved—or, better yet, exceeded—and there are no more campaign deadlines to be met. Now what?

## Celebrate

Take a moment to celebrate ... but just a moment.

Celebrating campaign success is important. If the opportunity to celebrate is missed, the magnitude of what has been accomplished can be lost.

It's time to bring everyone together and say, "Look at what we've accomplished. Look at how our organization has changed and how those we serve have been impacted." It's important to

> *Take a moment to celebrate ... but just a moment.*

emphasize that it was all made possible by the dedication and hard work of everyone involved.

I've attended hundreds of campaign celebrations over the past forty years, and there are certain things that set the best ones apart:

» **Demonstration of impact.** A team member talks with passion and enthusiasm about the difference that this success has already made and will continue to make for the organization, its programs, its people, and its future.

» **Personal messages from donors.** A donor speaks about what it meant to them to support the vision of the organization. They explain why it was important for them to give and how changing the lives of others impacted their own life.

» **Personal messages from those who will benefit from the campaign.** The personal stories of people who directly benefit from the success of the campaign can bring the vision of the organization to life as nothing else can.

Acknowledging and celebrating campaign success promotes a sense of accomplishment among all who worked so hard, and it can make board members, volunteers, and donors eager to participate in future fundraising projects.

## Show Appreciation

As I look around my office, I see dozens of items that I was honored to receive from nonprofits I served as a consultant, volunteer, or donor. They're expressions of gratitude for my efforts in helping them achieve extraordinary things. I have letters and plaques, posters and paperweights, a pewter plate, a carabiner, a Maasai ceremonial baton called a "rungu," and even a framed wrapper from a five-pound Hershey's chocolate bar.

There are big things and little things, and each one is meaningful to me. Each evokes positive memories of experiences and people. I can picture the faces of those who became important to me—some going back forty years—and I'm reminded of how hard we worked and how great it felt to be successful.

Achieving campaign success is an extraordinary accomplishment, and once achieved, it's important to make sure that everyone who was part of that success is thanked by the right person, in the right way, and at the right time. But it's not always easy to do. To help my clients do this, I've developed some suggestions for the best ways to express appreciation:

» **Plan ahead.** Don't wait until the last minute to determine how to express appreciation.

» **Don't break the bank.** It's possible to express appreciation in ways that are personal and thoughtful without spending a fortune.

» **Be thoughtful.** Use what you've learned as you developed and deepened your relationships with board members, leaders, volunteers, staff, and donors to customize the expression of gratitude.

» **Be timely.** A delay in showing appreciation can be seen as thoughtless.

The thank-yous that mean the most to me are personal. They reflect a knowledge of who I am and what I contributed to success.

# Steward Donors

In my interactions with donors over the past four decades, one refrain is a constant: "How come I only hear from them when they want money?" This is when an organization can lose donors—when they don't feel appreciated, engaged, or important.

I've had donors say to me, "Of course, I'll support them. I believe in them and what they do, but I'm not going to give them a big gift because they haven't kept me involved. I don't feel like my gifts are appreciated, and I don't know if my support has made a difference."

Stewardship of donors is one of the most important tasks during and after a campaign. An effective stewardship plan includes strategies to

» thank donors,

» recognize donors,

» facilitate meaningful engagement,

» promote fulfillment of campaign pledges,

» ensure that contributions are spent in the way specified by the donor.

Honoring donors and the commitments they've made to the organization is critical. Make them feel great about what they've done, and they'll be open to investing in your future.

> **Stewardship of donors is one of the most important tasks during and after a campaign.**

There is significant competition for donors. If you think of the donor first and hold them close, you'll build a lifelong relationship that is critical to the organization's sustainability over time. Investing in good stewardship today pays dividends forever.

## Thinking Long-Term

When I worked with a small conservation organization in the mid-Atlantic region, we had the goal of raising $10 million over three years. The campaign took a lot of effort, patience, and persistence, and about a year from the end, we realized we had enough prospects to win the campaign on paper. If we continued executing the plan, we'd reach the goal on time.

At that point, two things were put in motion:

> » We revised the campaign plan to focus on what needed to occur over the next twelve months and who would be responsible for making it happen.

> » We began to create the long-term fundraising plan that would begin the day after the campaign was over.

Here are the things we considered in creating the long-term plan.

**Case for support.** The organization would be fundraising for operations while implementing programs funded by the campaign. We had to focus our message on annual support over and above what the campaign achieved.

**Prospects.** The team had to create a prospect pool to reach its annual fund goal. Some prospects identified during the campaign were never solicited. There were current donors who would continue to support the annual fund at the same time they made campaign pledge payments. (During the campaign, donors were educated about the difference between campaign and annual support, and they expected to be solicited.) Also, there were still new prospects to be cultivated.

**Leadership.** After the campaign, fundraising leadership moved from the campaign committee to the development committee of the board. The board needed to steward campaign donors and provide assistance in raising operational funds. Also, the nominations committee had their work cut out for them; the campaign revealed several potential new members of the board and development committee who needed to be cultivated.

**Resources.** The demand continued for staffing, stewardship, and cultivation resources to maximize annual fund potential.

Developing this long-term plan gave the organization an opportunity to reflect on the impact the campaign had on fundraising. The successful campaign

» built the organization's capacity to raise more money every day;

» developed productive partnerships among board members, volunteers, and staff;

» created teams that worked together to secure some of the organization's largest philanthropic commitments; and

» established a culture of philanthropy that focused on fostering lifelong relationships with donors.

A big success generates the interest that keeps momentum and fundraising productivity going strong long after the campaign ends. As a matter of fact, the aftermath of a successful campaign is the best time to start planning the next one and keep the organization—and the fundraising team—moving in the right direction.

"The right thing to do and the harder thing to do are usually the same thing."

—STEVE MARABOLI, RECIPIENT OF THE UNITED NATIONS AWARD FOR PHILANTHROPY

## CHAPTER 16

# THE RIGHT DIRECTION

I'll be forever grateful for the training and experience I received at Ketchum, but when I returned to the company the second time, I couldn't help but feel my efforts to truly help clients were limited. Ketchum had created detailed service models intended to be implemented with little or no variety. They believed they had "cracked the code" and developed a system that ensured success for any nonprofit that followed it.

This limited customization, creativity, and flexibility, but it allowed them to hire inexperienced consultants whom they trained to implement the system exactly as prescribed. The consultants were evaluated on whether they achieved the milestones in the system. "Thinking outside the box" was actively discouraged.

As I thought about concepts for The Compass Group, I knew the service we provided must be different. I envisioned a firm where consultants took the time to get to know clients and had the experience needed to develop customized fundraising plans. I knew every client was different—there was no one-size-fits-all solution for meeting their needs—so many situations would require thinking outside the box.

# Thinking Outside the Box

As I built the team and the client base for Compass, I emphasized our ability to customize our service by sharing the following story, which clearly illustrates the power of thinking outside the box.

When my wife agreed to marry me, she decided to relocate from Iowa to North Carolina, where we were going to build our life together. As with any big move, there were many tasks to be accomplished. One of the biggest was finding a reliable moving company. This task fell to me.

I identified three companies and scheduled in-person estimates. The first representative arrived, looked over my wife's belongings, and gave me an estimate for the cost and delivery date—a five-day window eighteen to twenty days from the time they loaded her things onto a truck. While the cost was as expected, the delivery date came as a big surprise and posed some real issues.

My wife had accepted a new job that would start shortly after the move. She had a week off between her old and new jobs and wanted to settle in before she went back to work. I knew her well enough to know she wouldn't be happy about her belongings being held hostage, but my bigger concern was that her well-laid plans were about to blow up.

Recognizing that I'd be the messenger of this bad news, I wanted to be well prepared, so I asked the moving rep why it would take so long for delivery.

He explained that my wife's belongings would take up, at most, half of a full-sized moving truck. This meant the delivery timeline would be affected by several things: they wouldn't make the trip until they had a critical mass of items to deliver to the same region; the client whose items took up the most space in the truck was their first priority; and the time needed to make the drive.

As I listened and reviewed the estimate, I realized the entire business model for moving companies revolves around boxes. The estimate included a checklist of *boxes* for determining how many *boxes* would be needed. There was a diagram of how the big *box*—the truck—was divided into smaller *boxes* to accommodate multiple deliveries.

When I explained that I needed delivery sooner and a two-day delivery window, the rep claimed that was impossible and blurted, "It's not like you're renting the whole truck."

At that point I realized it wasn't impossible; it was just a matter of money. So I asked, "How much would it cost to rent the whole truck?" This stopped him in his tracks. He had never been asked that question and didn't know how to respond.

I asked him to find the answer and confirm that if we were willing to cover the cost, we would also control the delivery date. As it turned out, the difference in expense was well worth the ability to have that control. But to get to that solution, I had to get a moving company to literally think outside the box!

As the rep left, he said to me, "You know, I never thought of my business this way."

This is the kind of thinking the Compass team brings to every client every day, and I believe it's what sets us apart. Compass is more hands-on, more

> *We roll up our sleeves, sit down next to our clients, and say, "OK, let's figure this out together."*

creative, more adaptable, and more client focused. We don't just give advice. We roll up our sleeves, sit down next to our clients, and say, "OK, let's figure this out together."

# Getting It Right

Our corporate tagline, *the right direction in fundraising*, is more than just a play on words; it's a reflection of our values, and it's meaningful to me, our team, and the clients we serve.

So what does "right" mean? If you look it up in the dictionary, you'll find several definitions, but the one that resonates most for me is "being in accordance with what is just, good, or proper." There isn't one right way to fundraise. Getting it right takes experience, research, planning, a lot of creativity and flexibility, and, most importantly, hard work.

These are the hallmarks of Compass service, and our goal is to put our clients first and help them achieve their fundraising goals in accordance with what is just, good, or proper—*for them.*

This philosophy has helped us attract clients from every sector of the nonprofit world for almost thirty years and is one of the values that guides our work every day:

» We put our clients first.

» We approach every client with the confidence that "we can help these people."

» We care about our clients.

» We're the "good news people."

» We help make dreams come true.

» As with fundraising, our business with clients is all about relationships.

» We're not fundraisers; first and foremost, we're teachers, motivators, coaches, and mentors.

» We don't just give advice; we roll up our sleeves and work alongside our clients to help them be successful.

» We believe in creativity, accountability, and responsibility.

» We're all about performance.

» We know the difference between theory and reality.

» Our people are our most important asset.

» We believe in team.

» We don't just give advice.

» We strive to do the right thing for our clients every day.

» We play, and we play to win.

» We make a difference in the world through the work that we do.

# Democratization of Fundraising

Over the past few years, I've been passing the reins of the company I built to the next generation. In the process, I've been fortunate to find leaders who not only share my vision and values but are enthusiastic and motivated to have an even bigger impact on the nonprofit world.

> *The mission is to build the capacity of our clients to raise more money every day.*

They're taking the mission of The Compass Group—*to build the capacity of our clients to raise more money every day*—to a whole new level

151

and serving a more diverse client base in the process. The work being done is timely and impactful, and I'm proud to be a small part of it.

Compass President Rob Bull has a vision for the democratization of fundraising. This vision serves as the basis of a "blue ocean" strategy that puts Compass in a position to truly transform organizations and the people they serve through philanthropy.

There have always been the haves and have-nots in the nonprofit world. Not surprisingly, there are many more have-nots than haves. Those organizations struggle to generate enough money to fulfill their missions, and in many cases, they just scrape by. Often, they dream big, but they don't know how to secure the resources to make those dreams come true.

This is where Rob sees incredible opportunities to help organizations do more of what they do well, opportunities to set organizations on the path from needy to worthy, and opportunities for Compass to have impact.

Rob's "blue ocean" strategy has been enthusiastically embraced by the Compass team and has led to an ever-increasing diversification of our client base. It has also put our ability to think outside the box to the test. As Rob frames it, "This initiative relies on making fundraising counsel affordable and effective for organizations with limited resources, most of which tend to be organizations of color."

As with all Compass clients, the service varies according to the organization. But in implementing the "blue ocean" strategy, every team member is focused on

» being creative and specific;

» understanding the client's organization, history, challenges, and opportunities;

» determining the steps that must be taken to build fundraising capacity;

» recommending strategies that will meet current needs and position the organization for growth;

» setting goals that are achievable and lead to higher aspirations;

» being hands-on and working as a partner;

» wearing a variety of hats as teacher, mentor, and coach;

» demonstrating our commitment by creating a relationship that is both effective and affordable.

Needy nonprofit organizations have been underserved and misunderstood for a very long time, and Compass is proud to take the lead in addressing this issue. It's *the right direction in fundraising*.

"A good example has twice
the value of good advice."

—ALBERT SCHWEITZER

CHAPTER 17:

# FROM THE SOURCE

Over the course of my career, I've had the privilege to speak to hundreds of donors about their philanthropy and the causes they were passionate about. I've learned a lot from those conversations. Here are some memorable quotes that provided valuable lessons for me and the clients I served.

**From an individual in New England who participated in many local and regional campaigns and whose most recent gift was a $3.5 million challenge:**

"All the standard rules apply where I'm concerned. I have to know a lot about the organization soliciting my investment—ideally, over a long period of time—and I'm certainly more likely to support endeavors in which I'm actively involved.

"There is no logic to giving. Donors think emotionally—out of prejudice and preconception, out of knowledge and involvement, or an absence of both. Donors want an honest statement of fact, so the solicitor must be well prepared and able to make a clear, concise presentation of the facts.

"Interested donors want the best—the best colleges, the best hospitals. Show me how my support can make the organization the best, and I'll be interested.

"I want to be approached courageously and with no apology. Ask for the order. Be specific. Tell me what you want from me. Ask for a bit more than you expect to get!

"Most important, believe in the program and demonstrate that belief by your own gift. It will be evident to me through your words, mannerisms, and actions."

Lessons:

> » Make a brief, clear, and *concise case*.

> » Use *emotion* as well as facts.

> » Ask for a specific, reasonable, and *challenging gift*.

> » Use the benchmark gifts of others to *raise sights*.

> » Make the prospect *feel needed*.

### From a corporate president in the Midwest chairing his first campaign and making his first six-figure gift during that campaign:

"An informed volunteer is critical. Be sure you have an adequate command of what the organization does, what makes it different, what special role it plays in the community, and what contributions it makes to its field. The volunteer must be the one who sells the organization to me.

"Emphasize the voluntary spirit that helps improve the standard of living or the quality of life for my neighbors. The spirit of people helping people is a distinguished part of our American birthright.

"Do your homework first! Have a good idea about my personal giving profile. Learn about the policies and practices of my corporation or corporate foundation. Know the causes with which I empathize and why. Know what level of support is appropriate for me, and discuss that amount with me.

"Know as much as possible about the nonprofit and whom it serves, and have additional resources available. Those in charge of an organization should be a part of the effort to gain my support."

Lessons:

> » Know the campaign story; *know the organization* and whom it serves.

> » Sell the prospect on the unique value of the organization—*the case*.

> » Have the *right people* on the team.

> » *Know all about* your prospect.

> » Suggest an *appropriate level of support*.

### From a retired corporate CEO in the South who is a major philanthropist with his own personal and corporate foundations and a member of the boards of directors of several Fortune 500 companies:

"Fundraising is very competitive. More and more organizations come to me for support each year. It's becoming harder to make those giving determinations solely on the basis of a letter or proposal.

"Those organizations that are the most successful in receiving funds from me are those with which I have had some involvement— I'm an alum, a trustee, or a volunteer participant on some level. I believe in the inherent value and mission of these organizations. They serve a purpose in making this society a better place to live.

> **"I do not want to give you money; I want to invest in your future."**

"If necessary, send a contemporary of mine to make the ask— someone whom I respect—and I'll have a hard time turning them down.

"I do not want to give you money; I want to invest in your future and your ability to make a difference. Show me big plans, bold ideas, and dynamic leadership. Demonstrate that you're a good steward, you are fiscally responsible, and you acknowledge your donors appropriately."

Lessons:

» Have a *bold vision* and dynamic leadership.

» Demonstrate *good stewardship* and fiscal responsibility.

» Make a *personal visit*.

» Use *peer solicitation*.

These comments demonstrate that, if asked, many donors will clear the path to a successful solicitation. They will give you the information you need to help make their decision easier.

Finding yourself in front of a potential donor is half the battle—if they weren't interested, you wouldn't be there. When you're in this position, take the time to understand what they value in your organization, what they think about your plans for the future, who they perceive are the most powerful messengers for your cause, whether their philanthropic goals align with your organization's aspirations, and what might be an obstacle to a significant gift.

Take what you learn back to your organization, and develop a request they can't refuse.

Remember: Fundraising is all about relationships, understanding the needs and desires of both the potential donor and the nonprofit organization, and identifying a mutually beneficial way to meet those needs. Get to know your prospects, and let them guide you to success.

"Oh my, what a day
it has been."

—ANNIE ROSE CHEATWOOD PISCH

## CHAPTER 18

# ONE FINAL STORY

Throughout my career in fundraising, I've seen the power of philanthropy and the positive impact it has on those who contribute and those who benefit. I feel it when I donate to organizations I believe in, but I never expected to find myself moved beyond words as a beneficiary of the philanthropy of others.

Here's my own story ...

I had the privilege of meeting Joe Allen through the National Outdoor Leadership School (NOLS), where we both served on the board in the early 2000s.

Joe is one of those people whose humility and kindness seem out of sync with his extraordinary accomplishments and incredible career success. He's approachable and engaging and a great storyteller ... and he was an astronaut for nearly twenty years.

He was a member of two NASA space shuttle missions and one of the first astronauts to "walk" untethered in space. Joe is one of about six hundred people in history who have been to space. And ironically, he's one of the most down-to-earth people I've ever met.

Joe's awards and accomplishments are too numerous to be mentioned here, but they range from receiving a Fulbright scholarship to being inducted into the Astronaut Hall of Fame. He's the first to acknowledge that his career in NASA opened a lot of doors, and he walked through many of them.

> *I never expected to find myself moved beyond words as a beneficiary of the philanthropy of others.*

I'll never forget the time I was watching the film *Armageddon*, and suddenly there was Joe, full screen, counting down the launch of a spaceship being sent to save the world. I had known Joe for quite a while before this, and he never even mentioned it.

When Joe left NASA, he had a very successful career in the space and technology industries, eventually serving as the chair of the board of Veridian. When Veridian was acquired by General Dynamics in 2003, Joe found himself in a position to generously support the organizations he and his wife, Bonnie, believed in.

In 2005, the inconceivable happened in our family. Our thirteen-year-old daughter, Annie Rose, died unexpectedly. The pain and sadness of her passing is still with us today. This year we would have celebrated her thirtieth birthday.

As I'm sure you can imagine, people struggled to meaningfully express their sympathy for our loss. Losing a child disrupts our perception of the natural order of things and makes traditional condolences seem inadequate.

At the time Annie died, I had known Joe for only a few years, which made what he and Bonnie did even more remarkable. Unsolicited, they funded the establishment of the Annie Rose Memorial Garden on the rooftop of the brand-new NOLS headquarters in Lander, Wyoming.

Although I've expressed my gratitude to Joe and Bonnie often, it wasn't until recently that I fully comprehended the significance of their generosity for me personally. With their gift, they memorialized my beloved child, supported an organization I'm passionate about, honored my chosen profession, acknowledged my devastating loss, and created a beautiful outdoor space for people to enjoy.

Every time I go to Lander, I visit the garden. I go to the roof, I think of Annie and Joe and Bonnie, and I enjoy the view of the foothills of the Wind River Range. I think of Annie's joyous spirit and Joe and Bonnie's thoughtfulness, and I'm comforted.

I am, and will always be, overwhelmed by the power of their philanthropy.

*"If one advances confidently in the direction of his dreams, and endeavors to live the life which he has imagined, he will meet with a success unexpected in common hours."*

—HENRY DAVID THOREAU

# CONCLUSION

This book is a legacy piece—a reflection of what it's been like to have the privilege of working as a fundraiser and fundraising consultant for the nonprofit sector. The book is meant to provide insight into how I recognized the value of this work and translated that into a mission for The Compass Group that continues to guide us: *to build the capacity of our clients to raise more money every day.*

The men and women on the Compass team believe in that mission and strive to fulfill it with every client we serve. We believe in …

» **Service.** The nonprofit sector is at the heart of what makes our country great. It promotes character, grace, compassion, and innovation. Fundraisers are in service of values larger than themselves—the values of philanthropy and volunteerism. In this service, they help make this world a better place.

» **Relationships.** At the end of the day, fundraising is all about building relationships. Making fundraising personal, not transactional, can promote lifelong relationships that are transformational for both the nonprofit and the donor.

» **Capacity.** For many nonprofits, the impact of their mission depends on fundraising capacity. Investing in mastering the art and the science of fundraising can be risky, but when pursued strategically, it will provide great rewards, including a strong infrastructure, a skilled staff, and board members and volunteers who are partners working together to make aspirational, audacious goals possible.

This book is also a thank-you to all the organizations that Compass and I have been honored to work with—board members, staff, volunteers, and donors who are doing the right things for their organizations every day. They want to do good work, be successful, and leave something of lasting value behind. This is altruism at its finest, and it embodies the real values of philanthropy and volunteerism.

> *At the end of the day, fundraising is all about building relationships.*

As I shared at the beginning of this book, I believe I have the greatest job in the world because I wake up every day and work with people who are trying to make the world a better place.

There is magic in this work.

# ACKNOWLEDGEMENTS

During my career, I've been privileged to work with people who have become inspirational role models for me, both for their professionalism and the quality of the lives they've led. I'm forever grateful to have crossed paths with these incredible people.

**Ed Tomey** was a faculty member at Antioch New England Graduate School when I received my fellowship there in 1979. Ed's compassionate, insightful advice over the past thirty years has been instrumental in my professional growth and the success of Compass. He has perfected the art of listening and is an accomplished consultant's consultant. His partnership with his wife, Maich Gardner, is inspirational and enviable.

**Gale and Shelby Davis** are wonderful examples of what it means to be philanthropists. They've always believed in education, and, following their vision for international understanding and cooperation, they founded the Davis United World College Scholars Program. The program provides $50 million each year in scholarships for international students to attend colleges and universities in the United States. Approachable and sincere, they're great examples of what it means to give back.

**Elliott Oshry** was a vice president at the original Ketchum Inc. He was a trainer and supervisor for the consulting team. Elliott was the person who taught me the most; he always had the right words for any situation. He understood what our clients needed and how to provide it, while giving them the confidence to find their own paths to success. Elliott always put service to clients first.

**Russell Bennett** was the chair of the fundraising campaign at the University of Minnesota during my time there. Russ was a bear of a man; my hand seemed to get lost in his handshake. Devout in his faith, kind, gentle, thoughtful, and respected by everyone in Minneapolis, he was always humble about his many accomplishments.

**Steve Roszell** was vice president for advancement at the University of Minnesota. Steve's leadership during a tumultuous time at the university was a great example of grace under pressure. He later went on to have a very successful career with the company now known as Ameriprise.

**Robert Khayat** is a modern Renaissance man. He is a scholar, athlete, musician, and author. As the chancellor of the University of Mississippi, he demonstrated how one man with a vision and a plan could create a "Great American Public University." He transformed how an institution and a state were viewed and how they viewed themselves. He was uniquely positioned to make it happen.

I also want to thank the people from the "original Ketchum Inc." in Pittsburgh. When I joined the company in 1984, it was the largest fundraising consulting firm in the world, and it led the industry for sixty-six years. Those folks taught me the business and put me on course to find my calling.

I also want to thank **Kevin Gault**, who served as my writing advisor for this book. Kevin gave me valuable guidance from start to finish, and I'm grateful for his contribution.

Lastly, as I stated at the beginning of this book, the stories here are mine. They're my personal recollections of people I knew and situations I was involved in during my career. I've tried to be as accurate as possible in relating these stories, but in the end, they are my recollections.